FROM ADDICTION TO MIRACLES

Book Cover Design

The dove pictured on the cover represents God's Spirit. The calm waters signify the way in which God calms the raging waters of turmoil in our lives. The twig in the dove's beak symbolizes the new life addicts find through God and the 12 Steps. The red rose is in honor of my favorite saint, Saint Therese.

World Services Copyright Permission

FROM ADDICTION TO MIRACLES

By

Bill K., Jr.

COPYRIGHTS

ISBN-13   ISBN-10
978-0-9794424-1-4   0-9794424-1-9

Library of Congress Control Number: 2007901544

Printed in the United States of America.

Published in the USA by:

Keck Publishing Company
6908 Hartman Ave.
Omaha, Nebraska 68104

SECOND PRINTING

I am setting up the second printing of "From Addiction to Miracles" and it's been amazing what has happened since my book came out in October of 2007.

When I wrote this book, I reminded myself if it just helped one person it would be worth it, but I had high hopes. Now, a year later, God has blessed so much that I've had several hundred people thank me through the phone calls, mail and in person.

I've had friends and relatives give a copy of "From Addiction to Miracles" to their loved ones, numerous people have called for treatment or guidance, several treatment centers are using my book as part of treatment and the Notre Dame Sisters at the convent in Omaha have used it at a retreat. I've also had several Unity Church ministers use it as a meditation book and my friend, Father Schwertley, has purchased many copies to give for gifts. I wrote "Miracles" for several reasons:

1. To help alcoholics and addicts know they can get better and to outline a path they could follow.
2. Family and friends experience a tremendous amount of grief and I wanted to help in their healing.
3. To educate society in general about what addiction is and to help society understand there are millions of people in recovery today. And that is not an exaggeration! It's also a spiritual journey that anyone can take, regardless of their problems.

I hope you buy my book and spread the message, and remember that we truly can change the world, but it always starts with us. The Bible is filled with miracles, but I also see miracles all over the place, and I'm one of them. I am praying for you. God Bless!

To contact the author or order books, please visit the following web site:

http://www.fromaddictiontomiracles.com/

An alternate site at which you may order books is:

http://www.atlasbooks.com/marktplc/01828.htm#order

DEDICATION

This book is written in dedication to my wonderful, loving parents, Bill, Sr., and Shirley. It's only because of all you both taught us kids that I've been able to write this book. Thank you both for never giving up on me through all the pain and worry I caused you in the past.

I'm so grateful I can make you proud of me today, and through my life and accomplishments show what wonderful parents all 10 of us kids have. I love you, Mom and Dad.
Butch.

To all my brothers and sisters, I'm so proud to be your big brother.

Steve, thank you for literally saving my life. I wouldn't be here if not for you.

Allan, I'm glad we made it out of the insanity.

Bonnie, life's been tough and I miss Billy too.

Thanks really to all my brothers for the different times you had my back.

To my best friend from 1st grade, Gary Campain, thanks for discovering life with me and for being like a brother.

We all are so richly blessed.

ACKNOWLEDGEMENTS

First, I want to thank my daughter, Billie, for starting the typing of this book, and I especially want to thank Ms. Victoria (Tory) Stafford for taking over the job. Thank you for all your help.

Sincere thanks to Brigett Timmerman and Reid Kennedy for their encouragement and technical assistance.

For editing this book, I am indebted to Mrs. Jen Andres. Jen thought this book could be of great benefit to many and generously donated her editing time for charity.

My gratitude to Gerald Timmerman for believing in me and supporting this book.

Thank you to my children for inspiring me to get sober and to work so hard on my sobriety. I couldn't have done it without you. I love all of you with all my heart, and also all my grandchildren.

Thanks to all my teachers over the years that are too numerous to mention. I didn't just have to get sober, I had to become civilized to start with.

Thanks to Deann M. Ray, K-6 Art Education Specialist, Master's in Education, for her book cover artwork.

I also want to say I am so very sorry for all the people in my past that I've hurt and hope in some way I can make life better through this book.

Sincerely, with love,
Bill K.

IN APPRECIATION

To the Siena/Francis House and the "MIRACLES" Recovery Treatment Center, I am donating $2.00 from the total cost of each book sold. I hope it turns into a very large contribution.

To my counselors and peers, Frank Bailey, Linda Albrecht, Gary DiMasi, Rev. Chuck Cornwall, Tory Stafford, Brian Brown and Jason Reid and Day House Director Rod Bauer, I just want to say, "I really love you." Not very often, if ever, do you get to work with your best friends, but we do. What a blessing! Keep up the wonderful work you're all doing.

To the clients, "I really love you all!" You're clients and we're professionals, but the bottom line is, we're all doing this thing together. I'm so grateful to have such a team/family atmosphere to work in. Let's keep on making "MIRACLES" the best treatment center possible!

TABLE OF CONTENTS

PART ONE: THE JOURNEY

PART II: THE PROCESS

ILLUSTRATIONS

INTRODUCTION

My dear friends, I have a story to tell and I believe it can be very helpful, even life saving. It's my story of insanity, despair and hopelessness. It's also my story of peace, hope, serenity, love, joy and the miracle I've been given. I hope I can help you obtain your miracle as well.

"From Addiction To Miracles" is written in two parts: Part One is my journey from insanity to living life to it fullest and becoming a responsible, productive member of society.

Part Two consists of my thoughts on the problems, needs and solutions I believe in and also some of my personal therapy I've experienced that have and are making a difference in my life — a roadmap, if you will, through the changes in myself. I absolutely promise that, if you follow the guidance, directions and insights provided in this book, you **will** experience positive changes in your life. Your focus will become more "God and others" centered and you will learn how to dwell in serenity and peace. You will learn how to live, not merely exist, and your life will become a miracle for others to see.

PART ONE

THE JOURNEY

"HE WHO CONQUERS HIMSELF IS GREATER THAN HE WHO CONQUERS A CITY"

Proverbs 16:32

CHAPTER 1

WHAT IT WAS LIKE

"TO WHOM
MUCH
HAS
BEEN GIVEN
MUCH
IS
EXPECTED"

"NEVER, NEVER, NEVER, NEVER
GIVE UP!"
-Winston Churchill-

I'm a recovering alcoholic and hard core drug addict. I haven't had to drink or use drugs for over 28 years. November 22, 1978, is the most magical date I know. It's my sobriety date. Here is a brief synopsis of my past, which I'll get to in more detail later. I was kicked out of High School. I was an incredible athlete but never practiced or pushed myself due to all the partying. I've been dead twice. The first time I was shot and declared dead on arrival at the hospital. The second time I shot up some pure cocaine and turned around to shout to my brother Steve how good it was, and fell over dead from a cardiac arrest. My brother and our drug dealer tried to revive me, but the drug dealer finally told Steve it wasn't any use; I'd been dead too long. My brother shouted "NO!", jumped in the air and landed on my chest, which started my heart beating and my lungs breathing.

I've been busted several times for drugs and other crimes. The biggest robbery I ever pulled was in order to get enough money to afford a good lawyer. That lawyer took my case to the Nebraska Supreme Court and won, due to improper search and seizure. I was an extremely dangerous man. My whole self worth was tied into being the most dangerous man wherever I was and I would do whatever it took for people to know it. I've been in approximately 350 fights and sent at least 100 men to the hospital for broken bones, concussions, stitches and so on. Once I was shot and the defense attorney of the man who shot me brought nine witnesses to the stand during the trial to testify that I had brutally beat each of them. Each witness was over 6'5" and 300 lbs. The defense proved its case and the Nebraska court system declared I was a lethal weapon and extremely dangerous, especially if I'd been drinking. I'm not proud of that now, but back then, I was.

I've been shot and stabbed. My shooting was the subject of an article in the Grand Island newspaper at the time. The article stated:

> **Shooting Victim Hospitalized**
> A Grand Island man, William K. Jr., 25, was in 'guarded' condition at St. Francis Hospital here Saturday with bullet wounds received in an early morning shooting.
> Police said the shooting occurred about 4:30 a.m. at 2304 N. Sherman, a house occupied by Durand 'Duke' Ross.
> According to a police report, Bill was shot in the stomach with a .22 caliber automatic pistol. He was first listed in 'poor' condition at the hospital.
> Police said several other persons were in the house, where a drinking party had apparently taken place.
> County Attorney Robert Paulick said Saturday he was uncertain about whether or not charges would be filed in connection with the incident.
> Part of the decision would depend upon 'whether or not Bill recovers,' Paulick said.
> A police report indicated that an attending surgeon said, 'barring unforeseen complications,' Bill is expected to survive.

Toward the end of my drug addiction I was always just trying to figure out how much methamphetamine, cocaine, or narcotics I could shoot up without killing myself. I came close many times. I've been in many accidents. The worst one was when Crazy Joe and I were on our way to California to set up a drug deal and we decided to pull out our guns and play 'Best Man Wins'.

We were on a one way trip to hell when God intervened. For no reason at all, we had a one vehicle accident. The vehicle flipped end over end several times and then rolled several times. I ended up with a broken back, crushed shoulders and elbows and my spleen had to be removed. We had so many guns in our truck that the Bureau of Indian Affairs came to the hospital to question me. They thought we were running guns to the Indians because it happened on a reservation near Durango, Colorado. God saved us that day, like He has so many times; of course I just thought I was lucky or smart. My friend Crazy Joe died in a drug deal several years later.

I was married but never able to be faithful. I have wonderful children but was never able to be a good father, no matter how much I wanted to be.

I was a total mess and should have been dead or locked up in prison for the criminally insane but God, my Higher Power, truly intervened. I don't know why He lifted me up from the bedrock. I don't know why so many of my friends are dead or in prison but I'm alive and doing quite well. What I do know is a proverb from the Bible, "To whom much has been given, much is expected."

Today, unbelievably, I am the director of one of the best chemical dependency treatment centers anywhere. The Siena/Francis "MIRACLES" recovery program helps people stop and gain their balance, slow down, develop a direction and plan to reach goals. Our success rate is incredible. We deal with people who have been to treatment many times, been in jail and prison, are homeless and, needless to say, have lost all hope. Out of this incredible hopelessness they find themselves, as I have, being productive, happy members of society. I'm fortunate because I am a veteran and was able to go to a Veteran's Treatment Center and then to the ARCH Halfway House. Thank God we've been able to provide a treatment center for people who want treatment but can't afford it. Hopefully someday there'll be more centers like ours throughout the country.

"I HAD THE BLUES...
BECAUSE I HAD
NO
SHOES.
UNTIL UPON THE STREET....
I MET A MAN WHO HAD
NO
FEET."

-Unknown-

CHAPTER 2

EARLY CHILDHOOD/ DYSFUNCTIONAL BELIEFS

> **"I REALLY WAS
> THE TOUGHEST,
> MOST DANGEROUS
> MAN I KNOW!"
> HOLLIS SAID,
> 'BILL,
> YOU JUST
> DIDN'T KNOW ENOUGH PEOPLE.'"**

I'm so lucky! I'm the oldest of 10 kids and we've been blessed with the most wonderful parents. I'm going to share some early memories of my perceptions as a child about my parents when they were just two young kids themselves. My parents worked very hard to take care of us kids, so please realize I am very grateful for mom and dad and all they taught us kids.

My parents met when they were 15 years old, married at 17, and I was born before they turned 18. Mom came from a broken home due to my grandfather's alcoholism and my dad was a heavy drinker and a big bear of a man. My mother had a strong Irish temper and when dad would come home late from drinking, there was sure to be an argument.

For some time after I got sober I didn't remember much of when I was a child. Today I have many wonderful memories but at first I could only remember traumatic stuff. One of my earliest memories involved dad coming home drunk one night, mom getting angry and the two of them arguing. At the time there was only myself and my sister, Bonnie, and we were hiding behind the bedroom door. I told Bonnie (who was around three at the time) to stay hidden and I would do something. I decided to run across the room as hard as I could and hit dad in the leg with my shoulder to try and divert my parent's attention. It worked.

The importance of this story is this was the first time I remembered having a "black out." It was amazing, because I had a plan to run across the room but I didn't remember doing it until I hit dad's knee. It was fear! But I thought it was magical and wonderful -- blackouts would soon become one of my most prized capabilities...and later become my secret weapon. Whenever I was scared I would just blackout, go crazy and when it was over, come out of it. Later on I also had blackouts from drinking, and imagine how destructive that combination became.

Once when I was in about the second or third grade I sat down at my desk and reached in my pocket for my pencil, but instead of a pencil I found this little dart that you put a cap in. When the dart hit something, it would pop. I remember being surprised I had taken it to school when all of a sudden I saw it flying through the air in a perfect arc towards this big old mean nun's desk. It landed right on her desk and popped. Everyone in class was looking at me and I was trying to look at them but the nun knew who did it. She jumped up and ran towards me. I jumped up and raced out of school.

Why is that important? It was the first memory I have of a pattern of life that continued with me until I got sober.

I was always in trouble and wondering how in the world that happened. Trouble in school, in the Navy, trouble everywhere I went. I would get in trouble, go to jail and think to myself, I'm never going to come back here again. No sound is worse than a metal jail door clanking shut. When I got out, I'd forget all about the promise I made to myself about not returning. When that door clanked shut again I would think, how could I have forgotten? How did this happen again?

When I was married I would mess around with other women. I would turn around and tell myself, I'm not going to do this again, but soon I would forget and find myself in the same situation. I would also tell myself I was going to go straight home after work instead of stopping by my favorite bar, but time and again I found myself coming home after the bars were closed. I truly had good intentions most of the time but doing the wrong thing was more intriguing for me than doing the right thing. The closest thing I can compare my life to was like the little ball in a pinball machine. At a very early age it was like I got shot out like a pinball and just started ricocheting and bouncing from one thing to the next. I was never able to stop and get my balance until I got sober.

Sometimes the memories we have are accurate and real and sometimes they are only our mistaken impressions of what happened or what was said. Regardless, those perceptions are real to us. I have a master's degree in psychotherapy, and a two-year certificate in Adlerian psychology. One of the basic tenets of Adlerians is that our lifestyle is shaped and developed from early childhood experience. What we try to help individuals see is their beliefs systems and their helpful or dysfunctional ideology.

This next experience I considered my greatest lesson ever learned, until I got into recovery. I was in the fourth or fifth grade and stuck up for a kid in the sixth grade that some kids were bullying; consequently they got mad at me for defending the kid. They followed me home calling me names, and one boy Hans B.

beat me up about three or four times on the way home that day. By the time I got home I was kind of beaten-up looking, and the kids were still about 20 yards away calling me names. My mom was hanging clothes on the line and asked me what was going on. I told her I got beat up and they kept following me and calling me names. She got mad and told me to go beat that kid up and I said, "I can't. I already tried three or four times and he keeps beating me." Mom grabbed me by the ear and jerked me across the yard and hollered, "You go beat him up or don't you come home." I was crying and scared and wondered what I was going to do because I couldn't beat him. Then I learned that, if I don't quit, sooner or later the guy is going to get tired of beating on me and then I can beat him. From that moment on, the only way to beat me would be to knock me out and I've never been knocked out. Since that day, I've only lost three fights – once when I got choked, when I was shot and when I broke my leg.

Can you imagine that combination of total blackouts and the never-quit strategy? I thought I was unbeatable. When I got sober and was in treatment sincerely trying to get better, I once went to talk with my counselor really trying to work on my huge ego problem. I said "Hollis, I'm trying to be honest but I really was the most dangerous and toughest man I know."

Hollis thought for a second and said, "Bill you just don't know enough people."

CHAPTER 3

FAILURE

> "WHAT'S THE DEAL, DAD?
> AM I DYING?"
> "SON, THE DOCTOR SAID
> YOU HAVE A 20% CHANCE.
> SO,
> I FIGURE WE GOT IT WHIPPED."

In high school I was a very talented athlete. So good in fact that I really didn't think I needed to practice every day. The summer before my sophomore year, my family moved from Columbus, Nebraska to Grand Island, Nebraska. My old high school coach had sent a report to my new coach about how lucky they were because he felt I was the closest thing to All American material he had ever had. What they didn't know is I'd been drinking since age 13, and from that moment on I had lost the edge. I didn't realize how badly drinking had affected me until years later when I got sober.

By senior year the teachers had enough of all my fighting and troublemaking and I was kicked out of school. I thought it was great. I moved in with a couple of guys and we had a basement apartment with a refrigerator full of beer. I was cool. But then prom night arrived and my whole class was at a party out in the country when it dawned on me that everybody there was going to graduate except for me and this other dumb guy that had been kicked out too.

It broke through: I was a failure! I had never felt like a failure before, and I didn't like it. About that time my girlfriend and I got married. She was 17 and I had just turned 18. We were expecting our first child and I thought I could turn my life around if I joined the service. I joined up to be a Navy Seal but ended up in aviation working on jets. It didn't stop me from drinking though; in fact I learned to drink more heavily.

In Olongapo, the Philippines, we celebrated my 19th birthday. The guys surprised me and had a big party at a favorite night club. We got so drunk and wild we decided to throw everybody, except for our HAV 7 airplane squadron, out of the night club and down the steps. We smashed the place up and the shore patrol and the Philippine police came and arrested us and marched us onto the shore patrol paddy wagon bus. I got in an argument with the shore patrol and gave them the opportunity to get off the bus or get beat up. They left and we drove the shore patrol bus all over, picking up soldiers and sailors.

The next day our commanding officer was very angry and brought us up to a captain's mast court proceeding. As the charges were read off, they kept getting more and more ridiculous and he could hardly keep a straight face. Finally he said, "Boys that's the craziest story I have ever heard and the Admiral of our ship (Enterprise Aircraft Carrier) is really upset. We've go to do something so I'm going to restrict you all to the ship for 60 days. But we are leaving in three days and will be out to sea for over two months." Birthdays could be a problem for me.

I remember when we stopped in Australia, 350,000 people showed up in Sidney to welcome us. It was a hero's welcome. A short time later when we got back to the United States after being gone for one year, nobody came to meet us and certainly weren't proud of us for our Vietnam combat duty. It was a confusing time and of course a good excuse for drinking and partying. Not that I needed an excuse.

I'm very proud of being a veteran. I'm very proud to be an American. In the Navy I made a Mediterranean cruise, one around the world cruise, and two Vietnam cruises. I visited many countries. Until that time I had no idea how advanced the United States was compared to most countries.

I had a solid four-year career in the Navy even though I did get in trouble for drinking and fighting. Service men and women have a very, very special place in my heart. Thank you to all service personnel for protecting our country and fighting for democracy.

During my time in the service I had four children that I love dearly, but I definitely wasn't able to show it. Unfortunately, they were to experience a lot of pain, fear, confusion and anxiety in their early years due to my alcoholism, drug addiction and insanity. I am so very sorry for all the pain I caused my ex-wife and children, but I can't go back and change it. All I can do is the best I can today to be part of the solution instead of the problem.

After I got divorced I had one more child, a daughter from another woman. I just need to say that I love all five of my children with all my heart even though my actions back then didn't show it very good. Sometimes today, it's still difficult but I'm truly doing the very best I can.

When I got out of the service my drinking and partying progressively got worse. I wasn't able to keep a job and eventually started stealing, breaking and entering, cat burglary, strong arm robberies and so forth. Finally I decided I was going to change my life and I moved to San Jose, California. Later in recovery I learned that's called a "geographical cure." And of course it didn't work because, no matter where I went, there I was. And I was the problem.

In San Jose I became friends with some bikers, started using drugs, and learned how to deal drugs. My best friend there was a man named Dave who taught me how to sell drugs, and I watched him make a lot of money. It was magical to me at the time, but then, doing drugs was magical. I loved it! Later on Dave died from an overdose. Many of my friends died from over doses as did Janis Joplin, Jimmy Hendrix, and Jim Morrison during that era. The insanity of addiction is the total denial and inability to realize or care what's happening, and I didn't notice how crazy all this was.

When I returned to Nebraska, I found an open market, because nobody was doing drugs. I only knew five drug users at first and one of those was my brother. If it wasn't me, it would have been someone else, but I feel bad for my part in introducing so many people to drugs. At the beginning, I actually thought I was doing something great, because I liked using drugs so much. I thought everyone would enjoy it. I partied hard, more than anyone I knew. I saw myself as a party animal who nobody could hang with, because I would go for days at a time without sleeping, thanks to meth.

After I got sober, I realized the problem was I had lost the power to stop using. I had to keep using drugs, when others would stop and go home so they could go to work the next day.

I worked as a bouncer when I came back to Nebraska and it was at a late night party that a man shot me in the stomach and the bullet went out my back. Fortunately I survived, thanks to a very skillful surgeon. On the way to the hospital I heard the EMT tell the driver that it was no use in rushing....I was dead, I wasn't breathing and there was no heartbeat. It sounded like I was in a deep cave the way everything sounded so far away and was echoing. The driver said to make sure I was kept on oxygen because of regulations.

At that time I thought I was dead, and evidently you can still hear when you're dead. Then it was total nothingness. My last thought was, "Bummer, I'm dead and only 25 years old." Then I thought, "Well, I've lived more than most anyway." How naive was my thinking? I had barely lived by then and really had no idea what living was about.

Out of nothingness I had a flicker of thought that there was a noise and it was absolutely vital for me to hear, force myself to listen.......then it became louder and louder and I realized it was me gagging as they put tubes down my throat. I was alive!

When I came to, I was in the Intensive Care Unit. My mom, dad, sister and ex-wife were there. I had tubes going in and out of me. Whenever one of the women looked at me they would burst into tears. By their reaction I figured I was in pretty bad shape so, with what little voice I had left, I whispered to dad, "What's the deal, dad? Am I dying?"

Dad looked at me and said, "Son, the doctor said you have about a 20% chance of making it, so I figure we got it whipped." My father died on 9-11-98 and I miss him dearly. I love him so much.

The man that shot me really didn't have a reason to shoot me other than he was a hardcore alcoholic also. I wanted to hate him but I couldn't, because even though at that time I was in the right, my whole life was wrong. When the state took him to court the charges at first depended on whether or not I died. When I survived, they charged him with attempt to do great bodily harm and fined him $500. His defense proved that I was a deadly weapon, especially if I had been drinking. It took about a year to recover but of course that didn't stop me for long.

During that time I built a beautiful chopper and began dealing drugs. I thought I was doing people a favor by getting such good drugs. I even had three months on the job training program to teach my friends how to sell drugs and make money. Life was just one big party. At my first real civilian job, I worked at a mobile home plant and quickly rose to become the plant inspector. At this plant I was a bright and shining star. If I continued to progress, there was talk of someday having my own plant. For extra money I would also go out of state on service calls.

In St. Louis on a service call one time, I went to a night club with some friends. I was playing pool and hustling pretty well, when a fight broke out. I told my friends to get out and get the car, and after they left the fight escalated. I ended up jumping on top of the pool table kicking and hitting at least eight or nine guys with my pool cue. One of the guys managed to get on the pool table and I kicked him so hard he flew off the table, hit a paneled brick wall and flew right through it. My adrenaline was pumping and I felt crazy with power. Everyone was shocked when I jumped off the table and dove through the hole in the wall after him. I found myself outside and saw our car, but I also saw this huge cop standing there as well. He was a burly man, about 6 foot 8 and at least 300 lbs. I looked at him, we were only a foot apart and I was going to swing but I heard him say quietly and sincerely, "Don't do it." I paused for a moment and I could tell he was a kindred spirit and he didn't want me to get into any more trouble. He said it again gently, "Don't do it."

I looked into his eyes and said, "Okay, what next?"

He said, "Do you know this is one of the most dangerous bars in St. Louis? People get killed here. It's about time someone put them in their place."

I told him we were from Nebraska, just here to do some work, and were on our way home.

He said, "If I let you go, will you promise to leave St. Louis right now?" I assured him we would and he followed us down the Interstate for about 10 miles or so and we left St. Louis.

I do need to clarify something. The brick wall I knocked that man through? Turns out I sent him flying into the exact spot where a doorway had been paneled over. Back to Nebraska we went.

CHAPTER 4

BUSTED/SCHOOL

**"ARE YOU SERIOUS?"
"YES!"
"RIGHT THEN AND THERE, JERRY
AND I SHOOK HANDS AND SWORE
WE WERE QUITTING....
AND MEANT IT
WITH ALL
OUR HEARTS."**

I was totally shocked when I got busted for possession and sale of marijuana. One day I was with some friends and drove over to my house. Suddenly about 10 detectives, all in black suits, surrounded my car and prevented me from driving away. Everyone was very mad at us and took it very seriously. My friends and I were the first people to get busted for drugs in central Nebraska. I was placed on probation and my friends were either sent to prison or put on probation. I had been working at the plant for two years and, needless to say, I wasn't the bright and shining star anymore, but they did try to work with me by sending three of us to start up a new mobile home plant in Texas. It was exciting to go down to a large empty building and build all the stations necessary for a production line. We celebrated when the first mobile home came rolling out the door.

That day also happened to be my birthday. My childhood friend, Jim, had come to Texas with me. We went to an elegant nightclub and stood at the bar buying shots of tequila and bourbon. After a couple of hours, the bartender told us she was amazed at what well-behaved gentlemen we were after drinking so many shots. Happily we agreed and got ready to leave.

As we walked out, I held the door open for these two gorgeous young ladies coming up the walkway. I commented on how beautiful they were in a nice friendly manner. All of a sudden I heard this man getting out of a limousine say something about us being low lifers and to stay away from his women. When I told him to stick it, two of his bodyguards and the driver started to get out of the limo. I charged them, knocking all four of them out cold in 60 seconds and then piled them all into the limo. Jim was astonished, even though he had seen me fight so many times before and, once again, so was I.

This was a big mafia city and the next night across town after the bars closed Jim and I went out for breakfast. A shabby old man came up to our table. He said, "You the man that beat up those guys in the limo last night?"

I said, "No, sorry that wasn't me."

He said, "Yes it was you, cause I was there and I seen it."

"No," I said, "It wasn't me."

The man continued, "Listen, I'm not trying to start anything or get you mad. I just wanted to warn you. There's a big contract out for you because the man you beat up is the head of the mafia. If you don't believe me, drive down to this classy nightclub and you'll see that limo parked in the owner's parking space."

We drove there and, sure enough, the limo was parked there

This was a very old and shabby looking man, and there is no way he could have been in that nice nightclub 20 miles across town the night before. Looking back now, I sincerely believe he was an angel. We went back to our motel room, packed up and moved to a different city. Birthdays!

Since I was on probation, I had to see a probation officer weekly, but I was angry and sometimes wouldn't report. Years later, after I got sober, my old probation officer and I became friends. He told me he was actually happy when I didn't show up because he never knew for sure if I might just jump over his desk and beat him up. "You didn't get in trouble for not showing up, because I never reported it," he said.

I also had to see a psychologist weekly and attend a drug addicts group. This was before there were real treatment programs and all that happened was I met a lot of drug addicts and started doing more drugs.

My psychologist, Dave, always tried to get me to talk, but I wouldn't. I resented being there. One day he tricked me. I was upset about something at work when I came in he asked me, "Bill, if you had it to do over again what would you do different?"

I said, "I would probably go to college because everyone I work for is stupid!"

Dave asked, "Well, why don't you go to college?"

I retorted, "Oh yeah, how? I'm married and have four kids to support, plus I got kicked out of high school." Dave told me that if I really wanted to go he was sure we could find a way.

I couldn't get those three words out of my mind, "Why don't you?" Dave said he was sure from talking with me that I could do well if I really wanted to. Wow. I'd never, ever thought of myself as college material. In high school, when asked who was planning on going to college, I made a joke of it. I don't know how I came to believe I was incapable. My parents never told me that but somehow I had that message in my head

My wife and I got divorced about the time I started college. At first it was kind of a joke that I was going to community college, but I was getting good grades and on the honor roll. I completed a whole year, and then was busted for probation violation for being at a big party with about 10 other people on probation.

I sat in jail with my friend, Jerry, and felt really disgusted with myself. I told him, "Screw it. I don't care if I get sent to prison or not, this is it. I quit! I'm not even going to smoke pot when I get out."

Jerry looked at me and said "Are you serious?"

I said, "Yes!" Right then and there Jerry and I shook hands and swore we were both quitting and meant it with all our hearts.

About three hours later one of the jail trustees came back to the cell and told me he had some speed. I didn't even hesitate, I took it immediately. I completely forgot what I had just made a solemn oath not to do.

It wasn't until I got sober and learned about addiction and powerlessness that I found out what always happened was due to the absolute power of addiction and the strange phenomenal blank spots that block out all memory or thoughts of the consequences.

While in jail my lawyer told me that the judge said if I remarried my ex-wife he would put me back on probation. The judge also happened to be a Baptist minister and for some reason he thought I would be okay if I was married and settled down.

My lawyer, the jailer, several police officers and my dad all felt that, if all I had to do to get out of jail and not go to prison was to get remarried, then what was the problem? But I said, "Nobody is going to make me get married." After several of us who had been busted at that party (including my brother) got sent to prison, and I found myself standing before the judge who asked if I had anything to say, I told my lawyer, "Tell him I want to get married."

So my court case was continued and after a blood test they put me back in jail. After I got the marriage license my lawyer, who was also a Justice of the Peace, took me to his house and remarried my ex-wife and me. It all seemed like a bad joke, and I wasn't a good husband, to say the least. I caused my ex-wife a lot more pain.

She was a wonderful woman and certainly didn't deserve all the pain I put her and the kids through.

Unfaithful, unreliable and unable to hold a real job – that was me. I was just a hard core drug addict, dealer and criminal. I was very violent and had gotten to the point that very seldom did I just beat up on one guy. I became extremely good at beating up several guys at the same time. Everyone was amazed, including me.

Once five guys jumped me when I was with my wife and I left them all laid out, knocked out on three different parts of the intersection and driveway to a restaurant. An ambulance came and took those guys to the hospital and the police took me to headquarters. The police wanted to know who helped me beat everyone up so bad. I said, "No one was with me, and those guys jumped me." The sergeant said those guys were being brought back from the hospital and then they'd find out who was with me. When they got back the police chief asked them what had happened. One of the guys admitted they were drunk and rude to my wife, then they jumped me and I beat them up.

The police were always amazed because I was so tough and I amazed myself too. I couldn't wait until the next day to find out what insane things I'd done the night before in a blackout. People used to frequent the bars and nightclubs I went to just to watch me fight and hope it wasn't with them. I'm really not bragging, but I hope I get as good at something else as I was at fighting. I hope maybe it's writing this book. That's what I'm praying for.

One of my good friends was found in the back seat of his car in Kansas City dead from an overdose. I wanted to move down there and find out who killed him because I thought he was too smart to do that.

I just didn't know that none of us could see just how lost we were. I use to pride myself on what a good friend I was. I was loyal! I was the kind of friend that would die for you! Sadly, even though I was loyal, I didn't realize that I was a terrible role model to all of them.

Once a robbery I committed was described on television and in the newspapers as a very daring robbery. I admit, it was probably the strongest adrenalin high I ever experienced. After that, I noticed several other robberies were committed and in one of them an innocent person was killed. As messed up as my thinking was back then, I still knew that my example was what could have motivated them.

I don't know how I'm here telling my story instead of being locked up for life in a prison for the mentally and criminally insane. What I do know is, "For unto whomever much is given, of him much shall be required" (Luke 12:48). I've been given life, a wonderful life, and need to give back. I wish I could change the past, but I can't. What I can do is make a difference today. "Today" I can be a positive influence.

I hope this book will help make a difference. With God's help, we can change the world, and it starts right here, right now, with us, with me. I'm getting better and trying to carry this message of hope and God's miracle working power. The age of miracles is stronger now than ever.

DESIDERATA

Go placidly amid the noise and haste and remember what peace there may be in silence. As far as possible without surrender, be on good terms with all persons. Speak your truth quietly and clearly and listen to others, even the dull and ignorant;
they too have their story.

Avoid loud and aggressive persons; they are vexatious to the spirit. If you compare yourself with others you may become vain or bitter, for always there will be greater and lesser persons than yourself. Enjoy your achievements
as well as your plans.

Keep interested in your career, however humble; it is a real possession in the changing fortunes of time. Exercise caution in your business affairs, for the world is full of trickery. But let this not blind you to what virtue there is. Many persons strive for high ideals and everywhere life is full of heroism.

Be yourself. Especially do not feign affection. Neither be cynical about love, for in the face of all aridity and disappointment
it is as perennial as the grass.

Take kindly the counsel of the years, gracefully surrendering the things of youth. Nurture strength of spirit to shield you in sudden misfortune. But do not distress yourself with imaginings.

Many fears are born of fatigue and loneliness.
Beyond a wholesome discipline,
be gentle with yourself.

You are a child of the universe no less than the trees and stars. You have a right to be here. And whether it is clear to you or not,
no doubt the universe is
unfolding as it should.

Therefore, be at peace with God, whatever you conceive him to be, and whatever your labors and aspirations in the noisy confusion of life, keep peace with your soul.

With all its sham and drudgery and broken dreams
it is still a beautiful world.
Be cheerful. Strive to be happy.

(Found in Old Saint Paul's Church, Baltimore, Dated 1692)

CHAPTER 5

BACK TO SCHOOL

"SO MUCH PAIN MY EXISTENCE
CAUSED PEOPLE.
SUCH ANGUISH, ANXIETY, FEAR,
BETRAYAL, GRIEF, ANGER, SHOCK,
AND RESENTMENT.
HOW CAN AN ALCOHOLIC OR
ADDICT
NOT SEE THAT?"
"DENIAL."

I was 29 years old and tired. Once again, I decided to turn my life around. Since I had done so well at community college, I thought maybe I could go to a four year college, and enrolled at the University of Nebraska at Kearney.

I took psychology, sociology and criminal justice. I chose to take psychology and sociology, because I truly wanted to change, and criminal justice just in case it didn't work. I drove around with a carload of people smoking pot and told them to pick up any of those books in the back seat and try to read even one sentence. None of them could, including myself. I worked full time during the day and drove 50 miles back and forth each night for classes. Each day I wrote down all the words I didn't understand and my wife would look them up for me.

I passed the first year and got a job at the "Youth Development Center" (Y.D.C.) in Kearney. I worked at first as night attendant and then as a counselor. At that time Y.D.C. changed philosophy and went from a detention center to using "Positive Peer Culture." I really thought that was something but eventually I noticed most of the kids were still getting in trouble and eventually going to prison.

I had changed and straightened up a lot. I remember one time going to jail to talk to one of our kids and was thinking finally, I was on the other side. Finally I had changed and my life was going somewhere. I was helping others. I was proud of myself. It had been a tough journey but I had done it.

Little did I know it was just a reprieve. I soon was going to be worse than ever.

I stopped using and slowed down somewhat for about two years. Then one day my brothers came to visit and we ended up tearing a nightclub apart. We beat up the bouncers and the police came and I beat them up too. Then a second unit came in with riot gear and mace. They eventually got us handcuffed and taken to jail. Before they took me in the police station, the police slammed me into the brick walls outside of the police station. Guess what? An elderly couple just happened to drive through the alley and saw the police brutality! I've lived a charmed life. When I went to court all the charges were dropped because the couple had filed police brutality charges. With all sincerity, even though it wasn't right, I could not blame the police. I had not only physically harmed them, but I had injured their pride.

I don't know how, but I was actually doing fairly well in college. I was on schedule to get a double major in psychology and sociology and a minor in criminal justice even though my drug use began to escalate.

I drank daily and decided to do a sociology research paper on the psychology and sociology of go-go dancers. I finally had to quit that paper -- maybe you can imagine why. I used meth and coke on a daily basis and smoked a lot of pot. I used downers and narcotics to come down. I also got into acid, mescaline and especially liked canibanal (an animal tranquilizer like angel dust).

I was living a double life. I was married and going to college but I was not living at home. In Kearney I had my own place and basically lived like a bachelor. In fact some of my college friends didn't even know I was married with four children. Living that dual life seemed perfectly sane to me. To a normal healthy person it's unimaginable, but I lived it for years, when I was not normal or mentally healthy.

My existence caused people so much pain. I was sometimes vaguely aware of the pain I caused when I was right there but had no clue to all the pain I caused people when I wasn't there. Such anguish, anxiety, fear, feelings of betrayal, grief, anger, shock, resentment, and so on. How can an alcoholic, addict not see that?

It's called "Denial." The single biggest symptom of the "disease" of chemical dependency is denial. It totally blocks out any idea of the insanity of our lives. Without denial everyone would get better. They would have to. You could not stand seeing all the pain and futility without reaching out for help. Not only the chemically dependant person but their families also get caught up in denial of how bad it is.

In the Big Book of Alcoholics Anonymous it says the alcoholic was like a tornado roaring our way through the lives of others, which we were, but I think it is more than that. I think that we (the addict and family) were all caught up in a devastating hurricane called alcoholism/drug addiction that threw us all over the place and destroyed all that was dear to us.

I know without any doubt that I've always loved my family and never wanted any harm to come to them. Yet so much destruction happened!

WE WERE ALL CAUGHT UP
IN A
DEVASTATING HURRICANE
CALLED ALCOHOLISM/ADDICTION
THAT THREW US
ALL OVER THE PLACE
AND DESTROYED
ALL
THAT WAS DEAR TO US.

CHAPTER 6

GRADUATION

"DOUBLE MAJOR IN PSYCHOLOGY AND SOCIOLOGY TO CHANGE MYSELF.

MINOR IN CRIMINAL JUSTICE, IN CASE IT DIDN'T WORK."

I was set to graduate in three months when I was busted coming back from Colorado with some speed and several pounds of "Acapulco Gold," the best of the primo pot. It actually looked like gold. I had a friend who owned several acres of land on the top of a mountain that had a gold mine. He was a retired musician from the east coast. His supplier flew his airplane low to the mountain to drop off the pot. I bought pot and traded him for crank or crystal meth.

We were arrested on the highway near Grand Island. A friend had set me up. He'd given me $1,000 to buy some pot for him. It was an illegal stop and seizure, and they took my friend and me to jail. My car was confiscated along with all the pot, speed, and what little money I had left.

The only way I could possibly beat the case would be if I had a very good lawyer. With my illogical thinking I figured they arrested me illegally so it was justified that I commit a crime to get some money.

I robbed this place but I didn't use a weapon because I didn't want to hurt or shoot anyone. So I pulled off this big robbery and got enough money to afford a very good lawyer, I ended up beating the case. The state prosecutor's took it to the Nebraska Supreme Court, but I still won the case.

A couple of months later I got to graduate for the first time ever. Now I had a Bachelor's degree in psychology, sociology and criminal justice. Ironically, I was too messed up on drugs to be able to go to work. I was making quite a bit of money selling drugs and I found I couldn't make much money with a bachelor's degree. I told my college friends, "You have to be dedicated to work for such low wages in the helping profession." Little did I know that in a few years I would go through enough pain to become dedicated.

CHAPTER 7

ONE WAY TRIP TO HELL

**"WE WERE ON A
ONE WAY
TRIP TO HELL
AND
GOD
INTERVENED."**

"IT'S JOE, LET'S GO!"

I had a friend named Crazy Joe; he was a successful drug dealer and had a nice acreage, with Pasofino horses. He also had a very nice wife, for whom he had just bought a new jeep. He also bought himself a new truck. Life was great for him. He always wanted me to help him pull off a big drug and money robbery. I always said no. He had been doing this on his own for little scores. Then life came crashing down. His wife had an accident and after a couple days in the hospital the doctor had to remove her arm due to gangrene. Joe loaded up his guns and was going to go kill the doctor for letting this happen. I tried to talk him out of this, but he wouldn't listen. Finally I told Joe if he wouldn't kill the doctor, I would go with him to California to pull off this big drug and money robbery he had always wanted us to do.

We took about $10,000 worth of turquoise jewelry with us, as a front for having so much money. We took off for Los Angeles to set up the drug deal and then we were going to pull out our guns and basically best man wins. I didn't really care too much if I lived or died but I had been living a charmed life, so I figured we would win.

We were on the Sunni Indian reservation in Durango, Colorado on a perfectly clear day. I still don't know what happened, but somehow we had a one vehicle accident. We were on a one way trip to hell and God intervened.

Our truck was totally demolished like an accordion. Fortunately we weren't wearing our seat belts or we would have been killed. We were both thrown out and I spent a couple of months in the hospital. Miraculously, we both lived. We had so many guns in our truck the Bureau of Indian Affairs investigated. The doctor who treated me said he would like to know what really happened and what we were about because he was sure he could write a book about us.

Later, after I returned to Nebraska, I ended up having to chase crazy Joe all the way to a hotel in Hollywood, California to get my money back from him that I'd given him to hold for me when I was in the hospital. I told him, "Joe, I like you, I even love you, but I'm going to have to kill you if you don't pay me back my money." He believed me, which was good for both of us. He told me that was the first time in his entire life he ever paid anyone back

The last time I talked to Joe, I was sober and living in the ARCH Halfway house. Joe had just gotten out of prison and called me saying, "Bill, it's Joe, let's go!!" I told him I was sorry but I couldn't go because I was turning my life around.

Joe said, "No that's not what's been happening. We've just been resting, me in prison and you there. Let's go!!"

I knew the only way to get him off my back was to sound crazy. I said, "No Joe, I've turned my life over to Jesus Christ and I'm not going back." The phone was silent, and I said good-bye and hung up. Later Crazy Joe was killed in a drug deal. I felt kind of bad he didn't have me to watch his back.

CHAPTER 8

THE BEGINNING OF THE END

"WELL BILL, ALL I KNOW IS
BEFORE YOU CAME HERE,
WE DIDN'T HAVE
THOSE PROBLEMS.
SO,
I'M THINKING
WE'LL JUST
KICK YOU OUT."

My drug use got totally out of control after the accident. I got hooked on prescription narcotics I was taking for the pain. I began mixing everything: crank, meth, coke, Percodan, Demerol, Valium, Quaaludes, downers and alcohol.

Once one of my brothers, Al, got angry at me over some cocaine I was giving equally to everyone to use. A fight between us started when he tried to take the coke I had given to one of my friends. He tried to hit me and I threw him down and he tried again but when he hit the ground the second time, he came up shooting. Two of our younger brothers were with us at the time and the three of us ran out of the house, zigzagging as he shot at us. My brothers were still in high school at the time and hadn't been exposed to the chaos I knew on a daily basis. They yelled to me, "What's going on?!" We jumped in the car and drove to my house. We sat inside talking to my wife and kids, and then Al pulled up and began shooting at my house. I told my wife, kids, and brothers to lie on the floor and I got my .45 pistol and crouched next to the door frame and hollered at him that I was going to start shooting.

I knelt there with my gun in my hand thinking I can't believe this; I'm going to have a gun battle with my own brother. Thank God he drove away.

Things were definitely getting out of hand. I used to be able to keep the drug scene in hand by threatening to beat someone up, hitting them or choking them. Everyone was getting too screwed up. They'd rather take a beating than give up their drugs. I remember thinking I would either have to start killing people or get out of the drug business. "DENIAL" at its greatest. I could see how screwed up they were getting, but not myself.

Drug induced paranoia began to set in and I started hearing voices, people in the attic, behind trees, watching me and so forth. Once I tore the flooring out of the porch and was sitting on the dirt floor thinking I'd better get all the boards and the carpet back down before anyone saw it. In my college Economics class, I learned about supply and demand. California had crank/meth (speed). Colorado had cocaine. Texas had pot. So I decided to start trading and make lots of money. Then I started flying out to San Diego to buy drugs. Once I was in and out of a blackout that lasted several days.

I was in San Diego and went to the refrigerator and came back in the living room and said, "What are you people from Denver doing in San Diego?" I was in Denver. Then I went to the bathroom and came out and said, "What are all you people from San Diego doing in Denver?" Somehow I was back in San Diego! It was very insane and confusing.

I went to Denver to pick up some coke. My friend had several kilos of pure cocaine and I shot it up and fell over dead. It took me about a year to breathe right, but it didn't stop me from living this insane lifestyle. I couldn't stop. I was out of control.

My using habits had gotten to where I was always trying to figure out just how much I could shoot up without killing myself. Sometimes I would shoot up 40 or 50 times in one day. At times, I'd fall down, not able to talk, my heart pounding out of my chest. And my best friends were robbing drug stores. Drugs! Drugs! Drugs!

Finally my wife called my parents; they came to my house and knocked on the door. When I saw it was my parents I said, "Just a minute." I had to get a claw hammer and pull the 16 penny nails out of the door to let them in the house. I had nailed all the windows and doors down to keep out the cops or whoever. My family told me they thought I needed to get help. I excused myself and went into the bathroom and shot up all the cocaine I had left and flew back into the living room and said, "Sure, I'll go."

On the way to the regional center psychiatric hospital I reached into my pocket and pulled out a wad of money. I handed it to my mother and she began to count with some amazement. I had a couple of thousand dollar bills, a couple of $500 dollar bills and about 40 $100 dollar bills that I wanted her to hold for me. I scared her with all that money.

When I arrived at the regional center and began coming down from the drugs, I called my wife and screamed at her to come get me or I was going to hitchhike home. I threatened to harm her if she didn't. About an hour later, the sheriff came and arrested me and took me to jail for a sanity hearing set for the next day. When the jailer saw me he said, "Bill, what happened to you?" I knew I must look bad if the jailer was concerned. Looking wasted and weighing only about 151 lbs on my 6 foot frame, I was in bad shape. Normally, I'm about 240 lbs. of muscle from working out.

The next day at the court house my oldest son, Gary, who was almost 14 years old, asked me, "Dad, what am I supposed to say? They want me to tell them how crazy you've been!"

"Don't tell them anything," I replied.

Then my son asked me, "Dad, are you going to stop doing drugs and drinking?"

"Of course I'm going to stop after all this trouble," I replied. This time I meant it. I got out because they couldn't prove I was insane.

I couldn't stop. I went back to using as heavily as ever. One day a couple of friends were over, and we were at the dining room table smoking pot and watching my wife outside working on the yard. The following day, a Saturday, my wife complained about her shoulders and back hurting. I told her she must have pulled a muscle and prescribed something from my mini drug store -- the one I had accumulated from all the drug store robberies. After a couple hours, she complained about the pain and insisted she needed to go to the hospital. I gave her more of the Percodan pain pills I was sure would do the trick and said, "Take these, but if it's still hurting in a couple of hours, I'll take you to the hospital."

Later that afternoon she acted like she couldn't walk, so I played along with it and carried her out to the car. I was upset though, because I was certain she had only pulled a muscle. At the hospital they did some preliminary tests and while we waited for the results, I had her keep watch for the doctors as I went through the room looking for drugs. The doctor came back and told us they needed to do more tests because they thought she could have spinal meningitis and
she would have to stay in the hospital overnight. I told Dana I would go home and get some personal things for her and probably get some flowers.

What I did was in no way what I had intended. I ended up at a friend's house shooting up as much methamphetamine as I could and ended up on a three day binge and somehow ended up in Omaha terrorizing people that owed me money for drugs. I felt like I was only gone for a couple of hours, but it had been three whole days. I drove back to Grand Island, went to the hospital and found out she wasn't there. I was informed that the day I had taken her in she was rushed by ambulance 90 miles away to Lincoln to have an operation to save her life. By the time she got to Lincoln's hospital she was so paralyzed that she could only make an X for her signature.

When I walked into her hospital room she looked at me with pure hatred. She said, "Get out of my room. I don't ever want to see you again, you make me sick." I knew how she felt because I felt the same way. I made myself sick, and didn't want to see myself either, but I was stuck with myself. Here I had left her to go through something of this magnitude all alone; I also had left my kids by themselves. Thank God her parents were there to watch over the kids because I wasn't. The enormity of the situation was horrendous. I couldn't do enough drugs or drink enough to get any relief from the disgust I felt toward myself. I couldn't get high, no matter how much I shot up or drank. I went to the bar with my brother, Steve, and my best friend, Mitch, but I felt horrible, absolute depression and horror.

My mother-in-law and sister-in-law came over to the house and they told me I needed to go get help. I looked in my mother-in-law's eyes and I felt loved even though I had hurt her daughter so terribly and her grandchildren as well. I started to cry and my oldest daughter, Debbie, gave me a handkerchief and told me to go get help. I agreed and said I would.

All my brothers and sisters knew that I needed help and wanted me to get it. They all thought I was going to die. I called my brother, Steve. He came immediately and took me to the Veteran's Hospital in Omaha. On the interstate I told Steve I had some pot and gave it to him. After about 50 miles, I told him I had some crystal meth and gave it to him. After another 50 miles, I handed him some coke. And finally right before I went to check in at the hospital I gave Steve some narcotics I had stashed. Later, Steve told me he couldn't wait to get me out of his car and drive away so he could throw all that stuff out. It was late at night and they wouldn't admit me at that time so I had to wait until morning. Steve got me a room at the Holiday Inn and gave me enough money for breakfast and a cab (naturally I was broke). I didn't have anything left financially, spiritually, or physically. How horribly dark it is before the Dawn.

I couldn't get into treatment the next day due to a waiting list. I got a ride to Hastings Regional Center to stay until a bed opened up at the Veteran's Treatment Center. I was very difficult to work with and gave the counselors a hard time. I also upset the nurses. After about a week or two I was called into the director's office and confronted about problems with the nurses. I had them there and proceeded to tell about 10 incidences of unprofessional conduct by the nurses. I figured with my college degrees, I knew how things were supposed to be. The director listened very intently to everything I had to say and I figured I had them. The director, God bless him, looked at me and said, "Well Bill, all I know is that before you came here we didn't have those problems. So, I'm thinking we'll just kick you out." I couldn't believe it! My whole life I was always able to manipulate anyone I needed to: my parents, wife, girlfriends, boss, cops and even judges. But this time I was told they were going to kick me out, and for the first time ever I realized I had to quit the bullshit and change. In the past I believed my own lies, but this time it was either I change or leave. I made the decision to change and start a new life. I told the director I wanted help and would change.

Making the decision to change and actually changing are two different things entirely. I'm so grateful I had no idea how insanely sick I was because it would have been too enormous to consider.

I spent the first two weeks in treatment at the Hastings Regional Center doing two main things: the first was making a plan how to steal the antique grandfather clock from the cafeteria. The second thing I was adding up all the money that people owed me for drugs, which ended being somewhere in the thousands of dollars range. That gave me something to be excited about. In the drug world people rip you off for drugs, drugs that feed their habit. That's how the drug dealers like it. This way they'll sell his drugs for him to pay the dealer back and feed their habit. It's all a horrible circle.

As for the grandfather clock, my philosophy was that stealing was okay if you were willing to pay the fine if caught. If you got away with it, you earned it. There wasn't hardly anything that I might want that I didn't know where it was in case I decided to steal it. It wasn't until I got sober that I began to realize how much pain and grief people experienced when something of theirs had been stolen.

I felt very lost when I realized I couldn't steal anymore and really heartbroken when I realized I had to let all the drug world stuff go as well. It was all part of the disease and I had to entirely let it all go. I had to stay away from everybody, my old friends, my brothers and anybody else I had ties with from my past. I am a very loyal person and my friends and family mean everything to me, but I would have to let them all go if I was going to be able to stay sober and change my life.

CHAPTER 9

TREATMENT BEGINS

"WE MUST PUT OURSELVES
IN GOD'S HANDS.
WE MUST SAY TO GOD:
"HERE I AM
AND HERE ARE ALL MY TROUBLES.
I'VE MADE A MESS OF THINGS
AND CAN'T DO ANYTHING
ABOUT IT.
YOU TAKE ME
AND ALL MY TROUBLES
AND DO ANYTHING
YOU WANT TO ME."

I had been at Hastings Regional Center for almost three weeks when the Vet's Treatment Center called and had a bed for me. The program at H.R.C. was only 28 days long, I'd almost completed it, and I really wanted to go home. I was confused and didn't know what to do, so I got down on my knees and prayed. We slept bunked in a dorm, but I could never sleep because of all the drugs I had done, and was still going through withdrawal. This night, however, I fell right to sleep and I don't remember dreaming, but I woke up about three hours later and knew I was absolutely supposed to go to treatment in Omaha. I was convinced, and it became so important to me that I talked the night nurse into letting me call my mom for a ride.

The next day a friend offered to take me to Omaha, but I didn't have to be at the Vet's until the following day and so we spent a night at a motel. That night we stopped at a bar and I drank about nine beers, one after the other. My friend commented she'd never seen me drink so many beers so fast. While in H.R.C. it never once entered my mind that I might be an alcoholic, I just wanted to stop shooting up coke and speed. When Kathy mentioned the beers I told her, "Those guys are crazy up there, they think everyone is an alcoholic. It makes me want to drink more." I had no idea that would be the last time I would ever drink alcohol.

I entered the Veteran's Treatment Center on November 8, 1978, for a 30 day alcohol treatment program. I was absolutely depressed and hated myself. I felt I was worthless and a complete failure and couldn't imagine why I was even born. In fact, I was angry that I had been born.

Then I saw this big poster on the wall titled, "The Unknown Confederate Soldier Prayer." The prayer gave me hope! Maybe there was a reason for all the devastation in my life. I clung to that hope with the desperation of a dying man. The prayer says:

UNKNOWN CONFEDERATE SOLDIER PRAYER

"I ASKED GOD FOR STRENGTH,
THAT I MIGHT ACHIEVE.
I WAS MADE WEAK,
THAT I MIGHT LEARN TO OBEY.
I ASKED FOR HEALTH,
THAT I MIGHT DO GREATER THINGS,
I WAS GIVEN INFIRMITY,
THAT I MIGHT DO BETTER THINGS.
I ASKED FOR RICHES,
THAT I MIGHT BE HAPPY.
I WAS GIVEN POVERTY,
THAT I MIGHT BE WISE.
I ASKED FOR POWER,
THAT I MIGHT HAVE THE PRAISE OF MEN,
I WAS GIVEN WEAKNESS,
THAT I MIGHT FEEL
THE NEED FOR GOD.
I ASKED FOR ALL THINGS,
THAT I MIGHT ENJOY LIFE,
I WAS GIVEN LIFE,
THAT I MIGHT ENJOY ALL THINGS.
I GOT NOTHING I ASKED FOR,
BUT EVERYTHING I HOPED FOR.
ALMOST DESPITE MYSELF,
MY UNSPOKEN PRAYERS WERE ANSWERED.
I AM AMONG ALL MEN,
MOST RICHLY BLESSED."

In the "24 Hours a Day" book, on March 5th it says,

Sobriety can be a free gift of God, which he gives us by his grace when he knows we are ready for it.... We must put ourselves in God's hands. We must say to God: here I am and here are all my troubles. I've made a mess of things and can't do anything about it. You take me and all my troubles and do anything you want to me." "Do I believe that the grace of God can do for me what I could never do for myself? Hazelden. (1964).

I read and said this prayer every day, hoping that God would answer it. I stood looking out the window on the 11th floor at night, saying this prayer, "hoping!" He did answer me and has continued to answer, "one day at a time" for 28 years now.

At the Vet's we weren't allowed at that time to talk about drugs, just alcohol. It was winter time, there were about 28 guys in treatment and most of them were just there to get out of the cold. There were maybe six or seven of us that were sincere. On weekends we were allowed to go on a pass and when others came back, some of them had been drinking. I would confront them about their sincerity. A friend would visit me and bring some pot that I smoked in the hallway of the hospital at times, but that was different, I thought. I didn't think smoking pot was a problem and we weren't allowed to talk about it. Once again, I had no idea that was the last time I smoked pot. I drove around Omaha on a pass for a couple of hours and got really high because I hadn't smoked for a few days. That was 11-22-1978, my sobriety date. Thank you God!

I went to Alcoholics Anonymous meetings and I could see that this recovery program was working for alcoholics, but back then nobody was in recovery for being a hard core drug addict. I didn't know if it could work for me. A man, Cliff R., came to the treatment center and told his story. He had just celebrated his one year sobriety birthday. Cliff wasn't a drug addict but he had a hard core story. Every bit as bad as mine. I thought, "If he can do it, so can I."

CHAPTER 10

COMMITMENT/UNDERSTANDING I HAVE A DISEASE

> ## "I HAD
> ## BEEN
> ## FIGHTING
> ## A
> ## LOSING
> ## BATTLE
> ## FROM
> ## THE
> ## BEGINNING."

It was at that moment I made a commitment that I was going to do this thing no matter what. I wasn't going to cut any corners or try any short cuts. If this recovery program didn't work, it was not going to be because of me. I would take it to the bitter end and if it didn't work I would tell everybody to go to hell and die from using.

I stay sober "one day at a time" but my commitment is for life. If I were to relapse, I would come right back and start again.

I watched an older man (he was about 80 years old) get his five year sobriety chip about 20 years ago. He got up and shared how he had received hundreds of 30 day chips, numerous one year chips and had even received a three year chip in the past times of abstinences but this was the first time he had stayed sober for five years. He stated, "I'm a hard core daily drinker and I first came to A.A. almost 50 years ago. Even though I've had hundreds of slips, thanks to A.A. I've been sober much more of that time than I've been drinking. I would have been dead long ago if it wasn't for A.A., so I thank you all for hanging in there with and for me all these years." Wow, that was powerful!

I learned that I have a disease called chemical dependence and that, no matter how hard I tried, I couldn't stop. I couldn't stop the insanity. I had been fighting a losing battle from the beginning. I didn't know if I believed this or not but I hoped so because, if it was true, then I could get better. I'm so grateful to share that I found it's true.

I was trying to think myself into a better way of being. The problem was, my thinking <u>was</u> the problem – it was insane. What I learned is I needed to act my way into a better way of thinking. Don't try to figure anything out, just be willing to follow directions from others who have changed their lives. A reading from Hazelden's "Day by Day" book for January 31st says:

Living Ourselves Into New Life

"If we will thank our Higher Power each day for the problems in our life, we will find that we can live and cope with them. And if it be God's will, He will transform them in ways we cannot comprehend. We do not understand our lives.

If we will become willing to let God handle each of our situations in His way, we will find ourselves living ourselves into new ways of being. We will experience a freedom and joy which we could not have comprehended in our old ways of thinking and being.

We cannot think ourselves into a better life; we must live ourselves each day into better thinking. Have I lived myself into a new life?

God, I thank You today for the problems in my life, that I may use them to change myself into a new being.

Today I will live myself into a new way of thinking about......."

-Hazelden- (1998)

The Jellinek Chart of Addiction and Recovery on the next pages shows the process toward insanity and how an alcoholic's/addict's thinking becomes warped. The chart also shows the process we must take to experience recovery.

THE JELLINEK CHART OF ADDICTION AND RECOVERY

Jellinek – Part One

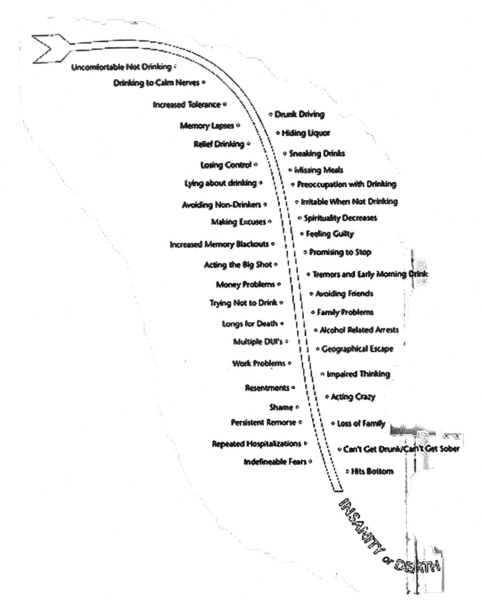

Uncomfortable Not Drinking
Drinking to Calm Nerves
Increased Tolerance
Memory Lapses
Relief Drinking
Losing Control
Lying about drinking
Avoiding Non-Drinkers
Making Excuses
Increased Memory Blackouts
Acting the Big Shot
Money Problems
Trying Not to Drink
Longs for Death
Multiple DUI's
Work Problems
Resentments
Shame
Persistent Remorse
Repeated Hospitalizations
Indefineable Fears

Drunk Driving
Hiding Liquor
Sneaking Drinks
Missing Meals
Preoccupation with Drinking
Irritable When Not Drinking
Spirituality Decreases
Feeling Guilty
Promising to Stop
Tremors and Early Morning Drink
Avoiding Friends
Family Problems
Alcohol Related Arrests
Geographical Escape
Impaired Thinking
Acting Crazy
Loss of Family
Can't Get Drunk/Can't Get Sober
Hits Bottom

INSANITY or DEATH

Jellinek – Part Two

• "Letting Go" as a Way of Life

Recovery Intensifies •

• Creative Solitude

Rationalizations Recognized •

• Prayer Deepens

Soulfulness •

• Awareness of Relapse Patterns

Daily Excercise •

• Peace of Mind

Ceases to Control •

• Contentment in Sobriety

Financial Responsibilities Returns •

• Sponsors New Members

Awareness of Codependency •

• Rebirth of Dreams

New Interests •

• Increase in Emotional Sobriety

Readjustment to Needs
of Self and Family •

• Healthy Diet

Values Develop •

• Ability to Laugh

Thinking Becomes Realistic •

• New Circle of Friends

New Lease on Life •

• Self-Esteem Returns

Seeks Therapy •

• Diminishing Fears and Anxieties

Prayer Begins •

Pride in Appearance •

• Natural rest/sleep returns

• Begins 12 Steps

Attends A.A. Meetings •

• Spiritual Surrender

Admits Powerlessness •

• Faces Shame

Realizes Alcoholism is a Disease •

• Gets Honest with Self and Friends

• Gets Medical Help Detoxing

• Calls for Help

...or RECOVERY

All the effort I put into joining the Navy, going to college, getting good jobs, etc. could not and did not work, because I had a disease. I had been fighting a losing battle! It didn't matter how hard I tried, my chemical dependence would eventually destroy any progress or gains I thought I was making. I've learned I need to go to 12 step meetings and develop a very strong support system of people with whom I can constantly check my thinking.

There are some very basic things I learned that help keep me sober on a daily basis:

1. Don't use no matter what.
2. Attend a minimum of three meetings a week [A.A., CA, NA, CMA, Coda]
3. Get a 12 step sponsor and call regularly [check out my thinking prior to action]
4. Read the Alcoholics Anonymous Big Book, meditation books or Twelve Steps and Twelve Traditions (12x12) book daily.
5. Prayer – Asking for knowledge of His will for me and the power to carry it out.
6. Work the 12 step program regularly [all 12 steps]
7. Reach out and help others (service work)
8. Write out Gratitude Lists

If I do these things I receive the wonderful "gift" of sobriety, serenity, joy, peace and humble gratefulness. The Bible is full of miracles but those are nothing compared to all the miracles I've witnessed since I've been sober, in myself and countless others. I remember in treatment when I actually could see people truly changing. I began to witness the difference in people at meetings from week to week. It was incredible!

My time in treatment was getting short. In the service when your date for getting out got close we called that getting short. You began to slack off, it was expected. So I started to slack off that last couple days and didn't attend group. My counselor came to my room and she said she was very worried about me. She did, indeed, look very worried. I was surprised and asked, "What do you mean? I've been doing a very good job. I'm the best patient you have."

"Yes, you've done very well up until now," she answered. "But now you've slacked off and you can't slack off in your recovery because you have a disease. I'm very concerned for you." I realized at that moment that I can never slack off in my recovery. I wrote her a letter thanking her for the lesson and wake up call. I'll never again slack off, I told her…and I never have!

I wanted to go home after treatment, but my counselors helped me understand I needed a strong structured environment if I was going to stay sober. I made a commitment to enter the ARCH Halfway House to get stronger in my recovery and develop a solid foundation for continued sobriety.

CHAPTER 11

GOD TOUCHED ME

"LIKE DAZZLING LIGHTS,
I FELT OR KNEW
EVERYTHING IS EXACTLY
THE WAY IT'S SUPPOSED TO BE
AND IT'S GOOD!
EVERYTHING THAT HAPPENED IN
THE PAST, REGARDLESS OF HOW
BAD, WAS THE WAY IT IS SUPPOSED
TO BE
AND IT WAS GOOD!
AND THE FUTURE WAS TOO GOOD
TO DESCRIBE.
TOO WONDERFUL
TO IMAGINE!"

I was filled with sadness, despair and grief because I missed my kids and wife. I went through severe physical withdrawals that lasted over a year, including diarrhea, severe migraines, headaches, flu-like symptoms and sleeplessness. I could only sleep about three hours a night and then had difficulty staying awake during the day. It was a nightmare, and something I could not have handled by myself.

I began to think I'd made a mistake and I should go home and try to talk my wife out of divorcing me (I had received divorce papers while I was in treatment). I'd try to be a good father to my children. One night I decided to leave the ARCH Halfway House, but I didn't have a driver's license or a car. I was trying to figure out if I should wait until morning when the phone rang. It was my dad.

He'd called to tell me how proud he was of me, to encourage me to hang in there. He said he knew how tough it was, and that he loved me. When I hung up the phone, it was a spiritual experience for me. I understood. Yes, I wanted to leave and go back home, but the truth was I was too screwed up to be a good father or husband. What I needed to do was stay at the ARCH and get healthy, so that some day, when my children needed me most, I could be there for them like my dad had just been for me. I was 34 years old, and never had I needed my father more than I needed for him to call that night and say he loved me, was proud of me and to hang in there.

My five children are grown up and have their own families now. I have a wonderful relationship with both my sons and my youngest daughter and just recently began to have the gift of a relationship with my daughter, Kim, and her husband and kids. Unfortunately, I still have no relationship with my oldest daughter and this truly saddens me. I love all my children very much and I know their childhoods were very traumatic for them. I have been able to be there for all of my children, at different times in their lives, but first I had to get healthy and sane myself.

A couple days after dad called, God truly touched me. I had just taken a shower and was drying off when this wonderful feeling came over me. I still remember it vividly: it was like dazzling lights, and I felt or knew that everything is exactly the way it was supposed to be, and "It was Good."

Everything that had happened in the past, regardless of how bad, was the way it was supposed to be, and "It was Good."

Everything that was happening right now at the ARCH was just exactly the way it was supposed to be, and "It was Good."

Not only was my future looking good, but it was too wonderful to imagine!

I couldn't believe this intense feeling. It was stronger than shooting up dope. I quickly dried myself off and ran to my bedroom to sit down and recreate this feeling but I couldn't. I realized I had nothing to do with making me feel that way. It was a "gift" from God because He knew I needed His love and assurance that everything somehow was going to be okay.

Today I'm living that future and it is unbelievably good! I wrote to my daughter, Kim, to tell her about that experience. It is difficult to explain the depth of mental anguish, grief and fear I felt at that time: wanting to run but nowhere to go. It was horrible; I used to go to church several times a week to feel safe. Once, I was praying and begging God for help when I picked up a Bible in church. In the Bible was a piece of paper with a poem titled, "Be Not Afraid."

Be Not Afraid

Based on Isaiah 43: 2-3
Luke 6: 20ff

BOB DUFFORD, S. J.

1. You shall cross the barren desert,
   But you shall not die of thirst.
   You shall wander far in safety
   Though you do not know the way.
   You shall speak your words in foreign lands
   And all will understand.
   You shall see the face of God and live.

Be not _____ a - fraid.   I   go   be -
fore you al - ways.   Come   fol - low   Me, _____   and
will   give   you   rest. _____

2. If you pass through raging waters in the sea
   You shall not drown.
   If you walk amid the burning flames,
   You shall not be harmed.
   If you stand before the pow'r of hell
   And death is at your side,
   Know that I am with you through it all.

3. Blessed are your poor,
   For the kingdom shall be theirs.
   Blest are you that weep and mourn,
   For one day you shall laugh.
   And if wicked men insult and hate you
   All because of Me,
   Blessed, blessed are you!

It touched my heart and I thought I'd get more to give to my
friends. I looked in several Bibles but none of them had that leaflet
in them.

What are the odds of opening up a Bible in a huge church and picking the one Bible in the whole church with that poem? It was God. He has watched over me so well.

When I was in treatment I began reading the "Upper Room" daily devotional and have continued reading it daily for the past 28 years. I even got my mom a subscription so we can share readings. I like it because it suggests Bible verses to read. This helped me realize that I had never read the Bible except a few verses here and there. I thought to myself that's insane; here I have God's life directions and I've never read it.

I've now read the Bible from cover to cover a couple of times and study it almost daily. It gives me peace and the feeling that God is watching over me and my loved ones.

Jesus promised to give us peace that passes all understanding. He said, "Peace I leave with you; my peace I give to you. I do not give to you as the world gives" (John 14:27). I've always believed in God, but not in a personal, loving God. Instead He was someone keeping score, and I was in trouble. I began to realize my concept of God was very small, very limited. I began to seek out how others believed and the fruits of their faith.

In jail I saw a lot of guys become religious, myself included, praying for help to get out of this trouble, etc. Now I was seeing something much different. I saw new lives unfolding and people around me truly changing. I could see the change in them and hoped and knew it must be happening to me too. I was seeing miracles happening!

"If anyone is in Christ, there is a new creation; everything old has passed away; see, everything has become new" (II Corinthians 5:17). God led me to treatment and the 12-Step programs to change me, so I could let go of my old self and become a new man.

CHAPTER 12

HONESTY, OPEN-MINDEDNESS, WILLINGNESS (H.O.W.)

"HE CAME AS A LITTLE CHILD AT CHRISTMASTIME"

"UNLESS YOU BECOME AS CHILDREN
AND LOVE ME AS THEY DO
YOU CANNOT ENTER MY KINGDOM
FOR THE DOOR IS CLOSEDTO YOU...
FOR FAITH IS THE KEY TO HEAVEN
AND ONLY GOD'S CHILDREN
HOLD THE KEY THAT OPENS
THE GATEWAY TO
THAT BEAUTIFUL CITY OF GOLD...
FOR ONLY A CHILD YET UNBLEMISHED
BY THE DOCTRINES AND THEORIES OF
MAN
IS CONTENT TO TRUST AND LOVE
JESUS WITHOUT UNDERSTANDING
HIS PLAN.

-Helen Steiner Rice-

These three principles are indispensable if we want to change: Honesty, Open-mindedness and Willingness. It seems ridiculous to me now, but I actually thought I was an honest person and didn't lie. I learned the importance of being honest early on, because I almost used, and would have except for God's grace. It's kind of an embarrassing story, but when I was sober about four months, I had an old girlfriend call me from Colorado to say she was coming to Nebraska and wanted to see me. She would only be able to see me for a couple of hours in the early afternoon and would stop by work. It would be nice to see her because she was a good friend and I missed some of my old friends. Even though my wife was divorcing me, I told all the guys in my halfway house that I wanted to be faithful to her, because in the past I'd been so unfaithful, so they helped me.

Well, my friend and I used to have great sex and I started thinking about what might happen during her visit. Since she would only be here during work hours, we might have sex, but if I told the guys they'd remind me of my plan to stay faithful, so I didn't tell them. It wasn't lying, but it was. I was being sneaky about her visit.

My main coke dealer in Boulder, Colorado had sent drugs down with her for me. Soon after she arrived, I told her how sincere I was about recovery and going home and being a good father. Then she handed me a vial of a beautiful rock of coke. She'd saved a syringe needle, but couldn't find the needle. She said. "I looked all through the car three times, but can't find it."

An incredible thing happened then: my mind filled with a picture of about 50 of my friends and my brother, Steve, with a pool cue in his hands, all happy and beckoning me to come. I said, "It's a good thing you couldn't find the needle or I'd shoot this up." The only way I ever got high with coke was from shooting it up, so I was able to give it back to her.

The next day I shared this in our group therapy and all 12 guys were very shaken that this had happened to me because everyone knew how serious and hard a program I worked. The counselor, John, said I must have set myself up, but all of us guys attested to how diligent a program I worked. John said, "Let's go back over the past week or two and see where you (my disease) set this relapse process up."

Of course we realized it was when I made a decision to be dishonest by omission. That has been such a wonderful, meaningful experience for me. I was so blessed to be given that lesson without having to use. I truly, absolutely believe that God took that syringe.

I believe every alcoholic and addict experiences a life and death lesson early in recovery and if we heed it and learn the lesson, it will keep us sober. My lesson was that my sobriety is completely dependent on my honesty.

I also thought I was open-minded. In fact, throughout my life I'd prided myself on how open-minded I was. Mom and dad picked me up and along with my siblings we went to visit my sister Kathy living in Memphis. We were all in the kitchen and Kathy exclaimed, "This is wonderful it's the first time we've ever talked." "What are you talking about?" I replied "We always talked." She said, "No, in the past you talked and I listened but this is the first time I ever felt you listening to me." I didn't understand.

About a year later my dad told me, "I really enjoy talking to you son. Several years ago I quit telling you what I thought because you wouldn't listen. Instead you would tell me I was wrong and how you were right."

This was difficult and painful to hear. People I loved and cared about were telling me how closed-minded I had been in the past years. What's even worse is I was so self-centered I didn't even notice. Self-centeredness is the main characteristic of a chemically dependent person.

The third principle is Willingness. I had to forget everything I thought I knew. I remember telling someone, "It's so basic I'm going to have to start with learning to tie my shoes over." I had to be willing to turn my entire life over to God and trust that He was working through the people He had placed in my life. The main confrontation I had at the Vet's treatment was that I didn't trust anybody. Thanks to treatment I learned that the person I could trust least of all was me. I was by far my worst enemy!

I once had a poster of two identical cats skipping down the road and it said, "Be your own best friend." The message was not to do what I wanted for short term gratification, but to do what would be best for me down the road, next week, next month, next year, and so on. Today, I can say I've been my own best friend for 28 years now.

CHAPTER 13

"HOW IT WORKS"

"I'VE
BEEN
BORN
AGAIN,
ROCKETED
INTO
A
FOURTH
DIMENSION"

The Bible spells out how mankind should live and it's all in there. All the directions for a happy, God-filled life are there. But I needed it broken down even more. Many people are "born again," and my prayer is that every single soul be "born again," however that happens.

I went to several different churches and walked down the aisle to be prayed over to be "born again." Nothing happened. I could see by the bright smiles and peace on peoples' faces that something truly was happening for them, but it didn't happen for me. I felt even more hopeless and depressed.

I've found out why it didn't happen for me then: because it was supposed to happen for me at 12-Step meetings. That is when the light came on in my eyes. That is where I found God.

I was born Catholic and always believed in God, so I thought. But I didn't really feel God in my life or learn to truly let God guide my life. Jesus is my Savior. I honestly have let Him remove my old self and put on my new self. Today, I'm able to be a good Catholic, but it started for me in A.A. However, I totally believe He comes to people in many different ways and religions.

From the Alcoholics Anonymous book, I'm going to quote three pages that simplified the Bible in terms I could understand.

> Rarely have we seen a person fail who has thoroughly followed our path. Those who do not recover are people who cannot or will not completely give themselves to this simple program, usually men and women who are constitutionally incapable of being honest with themselves. There are such unfortunates. They are not at fault; they seem to have been born that way. They are naturally incapable of grasping and developing a manner of living which demands rigorous honesty. Their chances are less than average. There are those, too, who suffer from grave emotional and mental disorders, but many of them do recover if they have the capacity to be honest.
>
> Our stories disclose in a general way what we used to be like, what happened, and what we are like now. If you have decided you want what we have and are willing to go to any length to get it – then you are ready to take certain steps.

At some of these, we balked. We thought we could find an easier, softer way. But we could not. With all the earnestness at our command, we beg of you to be fearless and thorough from the very start. Some of us have tried to hold on to our old ideas and the result was nil until we leg go absolutely.

Remember that we deal with alcohol – cunning, baffling, powerful! Without help it is too much for us. But there is One who has all power – that One is God. May you find Him now!

Half measures availed us nothing. We stood at the turning point. We asked His protection and care with complete abandon.

Here are the steps we took, which are suggested as a program of recovery:

1. We admitted we were powerless over alcohol – that our lives had become unmanageable.
2. Came to believe that a Power greater than ourselves could restore us to sanity.
3. Made a decision to turn our will and our lives over to the care of God as we understood Him.
4. Made a searching and fearless moral inventory of ourselves.
5. Admitted to God, to ourselves, and to another human being the exact nature of our wrongs.
6. Were entirely ready to have God remove all these defects of character.
7. Humbly asked Him to remove our shortcomings.
8. Made a list of all persons we had harmed, and became willing to make amends to them all.
9. Made direct amends to such people wherever possible, except when to do so would injure them or others.
10. Continued to take personal inventory and when we were wrong promptly admitted it.
11. Sought through prayer and meditation to improve our conscious contact with God as we understood Him, praying

only for knowledge of His will for us and the power to carry that out.

12. Having had a spiritual awakening as the result of these steps, we tried to carry this message to alcoholics, and to practice these principles in all our affairs.

Many of us exclaimed, "What an order! I can't go through with it." Do not be discouraged. No one among us has been able to maintain anything like perfect adherence to these principles. We are not saints. The point is that we are willing to grow along spiritual lines. The principles we have set down are guides to progress. We claim spiritual progress rather than spiritual perfection.

Our description of the alcoholic, the chapter to the agnostic, and our personal adventures before and after makes clear three pertinent ideas:

a) That we were alcoholic and could not manage our own lives.

b) That probably no human power could have relieved our alcoholism.

c) That God could and would if He were sought.

Being convinced, we were at Step Three, which is that we decided to turn our will and our life over to God as we understood Him. Just what do we mean by that, and just what do we do?

The first requirement is that we be convinced that any life run on self-will can hardly be a success. On that basis we are almost always in collision with something or somebody, even though our motives are good. Most people try to live by self-propulsion. Each person is like an actor who wants to run the whole show, is forever trying to arrange the lights, the ballet, the scenery and the rest of the players in his own way. If his arrangements would only stay put, if only people would do as he wished, the show would be great. Everybody, including himself, would be pleased. Life would be wonderful. In trying to make these arrangements our actor may sometimes be quite virtuous. He may be kind, considerate, patient, generous; even modest and self-sacrificing. On the other hand, he may be mean, egotistical, selfish and dishonest. But, as with most humans, he is more likely to have varied traits.

What usually happens? The show doesn't come off very well. He begins to think life doesn't treat him right. He decides to exert himself more. He becomes, on the next occasion, still more demanding or gracious, as the case may be. Still the play does not suit him. Admitting he may be somewhat at fault, he is sure that other people are more to blame. He becomes angry, indignant, self-pitying. What is his basic trouble? Is he not really a self-seeker even when trying to be kind? Is he not a victim of the delusion that he can wrest satisfaction and happiness out of his world if he only manages well? Is it not evident to all the rest of the players that these are the things he wants? And do not his actions make each of them wish to retaliate, snatching all they can get out of the show? Is he not, even in his best moments, a producer of confusion, rather than harmony?

Our actor is self-centered – ego-centric, people like to call it nowadays. He is like the retired businessman who lolls in the Florida sunshine in the winter, complaining of the sad state of the nation; the minister who sighs over the sins of the twentieth century; politicians and reformers who are sure all would be Utopia if the rest of the world would only behave; the outlaw safe cracker who thinks society has wronged him; and the alcoholic who has lost all and is locked up. Whatever our protestations, are not most of us concerned with ourselves, our resentments or our self pity?

Selfishness – self-centeredness! That, we think, is the root of our troubles. Driven by a hundred forms of fear, self-delusion, self-seeking and self-pity, we step on the toes of our fellows and they retaliate. Sometimes they hurt us, seemingly without provocation, but we invariably find that at some time in the past we have made decisions based on self which later placed us a position to be hurt.

So our troubles, we think, are basically of our own making. They arise out of ourselves, and the alcoholic is an extreme example of self-will run riot, though he usually doesn't think so. Above everything, we alcoholics must be rid of this selfishness. We must, or it kills us! God makes that possible. And there often seems no way of entirely getting rid of self without His aid. Many of us had moral and philosophical convictions galore, but we could not live up to them even though we would have liked to. Neither could we reduce our self-centeredness much by wishing or trying on our own power. We had to have God's help.

This is the how and why of it. First of all, we had to quit playing God. It didn't work. Next, we decided that hereafter in this drama of life, God was going to be our Director. He is the Principal; we are His agents. He is the Father, and we are His children. Most good ideas are simple, and this concept was the keystone of the new and triumphant arch through which we passed to freedom.

When we sincerely took such a position, all sorts of remarkable things followed. We had a new Employer. Being all powerful, He provided what we needed, if we kept close to Him and performed His work well. Established on such a footing we became less and less interested in ourselves, our little plans and designs. More and more we became interested in seeing what we could contribute to life. As we felt new power flow in, as we enjoyed peace of mind, as we discovered we could face life successfully, as we began to lose our fear of today, tomorrow or the hereafter. We were reborn.

We were now at Step Three. Many of us said to our Maker, as we understood Him: "God, I offer myself to Thee—to build with me and to do with me as Thou wilt. Relieve me of the bondage of self, that I may better do Thy will. Take away my difficulties, that victory over them may bear witness to those I would help of Thy Power, Thy Love and Thy Way of life. May I do Thy will always!" We thought well before taking this step making sure we were ready; that we could at last abandon ourselves utterly to Him. A.A. Big Book 58-60.

I have been born again. I've been rocketed into a fourth dimension that I never knew existed. These pages are some of my favorites, but really the entire book is filled with such basic and simple knowledge. What is also so amazing is that no matter what the problem, the solution always involves looking at ourselves. I need to recognize what must change in me, my attitudes and beliefs, etc. so that I can experience peace and serenity.

I sincerely recommend that everyone buy a copy of the Big Book of Alcoholics Anonymous and read it. Of all the books I read in college and during therapist certification, none match the Big Book's incredible wealth of knowledge for self transformation.

CHAPTER 14

HOUSEKEEPER

"I STOOD AT
AN INTERSECTION
IN A SNOWSTORM, AND
EVERYONE DRIVING BY LOOKED
LIKE THEY HAD A PURPOSE IN
LIFE.
EVERYONE
WAS GOING SOMEWHERE.
CARS, TRUCKS, CADILLACS,
VOLKSWAGENS.
THEY ALL HAD LIVES."

At the ARCH Halfway House, we had to have a job within two weeks or be asked to leave. A temp agency found me my first job, as a spot laborer unloading lumber from a boxcar. It was a freezing winter, and although I had a coat I'd stolen from the Vet's Hospital, I had no gloves. An old homeless man I worked with gave me a hole-filled pair of gloves and I was very grateful.

The job gave me enough money to take the bus, so I could put in applications for another job. Soon I was broke and only had enough money ($.35) for a one-way ticket on the bus. Luther, a roommate at ARCH, and I took the bus as far as it would take us to put in an application. We had to walk about a mile further in a very heavy snowfall to get there.

We didn't even get to talk with anyone; I just submitted the application and they said they would call. As we walked back to the bus stop, I rehearsed how to ask Luther for $.35 to take the bus. I was so ashamed.

We stood at the bus stop in the middle of a snowstorm with all these cars going by and everyone looked like they had a purpose in life. Everyone was going somewhere. Cars, trucks, dump trucks, Cadillacs, Volkswagens….they all had lives. I stood there trying to get up enough nerve to ask for $.35. I felt hopeless, worthless and depressed. And I felt scared. I finally asked Luther for the bus fare and he happily gave it to me. Still, it didn't lessen my feelings of worthlessness.

In the process of looking for a job, I heard about this guy, Whitey, who was an assistant manager at a nursing home and he was moving out of state. I thought I'd go apply and put my education to work. I applied and was hired, but not as assistant manager. I, Bill K., the meanest, baddest, big time dope dealer, had been hired as a housekeeper. I had to take the job, because my two weeks were up.

It was depressing. My job was cleaning the toilets (about 40 of them). Can you believe it? God actually got me a job where I had to be on my hands and knees, scrubbing out toilets.

How humbling, and I needed to be humbled. I didn't know how to work and stay at a job. I had to find meaning in this job if I was going to make it. I decided I was going to clean these toilets and bathrooms and have them sparkling for God.

One day all the other people who worked as housekeepers confronted me. "What are you doing?" they asked. "You're making us look bad, working that hard."

I told them, "I'm sorry, but I don't know what's working hard or not. I'm just working as hard as I can." God handpicked that job for me to learn how to work and to find meaning in my work.

After four months, I was promoted to janitor. One day I was mopping and waxing the front lobby area and I found myself worrying about someone walking in and seeing me mopping the floor. When I was cleaning the bathrooms, at least no one saw me. Now I was out in the open. This was my "false pride" in operation – thinking I was too good to be scrubbing the floors.

I needed a lot of work on humility. I now have a miniature desk with a chalkboard with a little Buddha on my desk and the Buddha says, "Humility is teachability." Some days I have it pointed toward my clients. Some days I have it pointed towards me. Sometimes it is pointed where we all can see it. It is an ongoing effort.

After five months as a janitor, I was promoted to maintenance man. One of my first days on the job, I noticed the big magnetic lock on the backdoor was broken. I thought, "Someone needs to fix that." I'd forgotten I was the maintenance man. I've always been mechanically inclined, but when I began to tear the lock apart. I thought, "What if I can't put this back together!" It was a real crippling fear, until I remembered what I had been learning in recovery....It's okay to ask for help. Wow, yeah, I can ask for help and it's okay to do so. I was so happy to have learned that. Without it, I couldn't do the work I do today; I couldn't develop treatment centers or work with an extremely diverse group of clients if I hadn't learned that lesson that day. "It's okay to ask for help."

After working as a maintenance man for about six months, management decided to change the Omaha Manor from a nursing home to a home and school for mentally retarded clients. My boss was impressed with my work, and how well I was able to respond to the clients and he was aware of my education. He encouraged me to apply for the therapist opening and I did. I was then promoted to being a therapist for the mentally retarded. It's incredible what plans God has for us when we allow Him to run the show. And He has these plans for every single one of us when we learn to live spiritually.

A couple other major events that happened during this time involved my boss, Pete, a recovering alcoholic. He wanted to set aside nine beds for hardcore, hopeless alcoholics. I developed the treatment program. It was my first treatment program and it planted the seed for helping all those who couldn't afford treatment and, ultimately, the "MIRACLES" Treatment Center.

I began training to be a certified alcohol and drug counselor.

CHAPTER 15

COUNSELOR TRAINING

"PEOPLE PRAY TO
GOD ALMIGHTY,
ASKING FOR HIS HELP
AND HE HELPS THEM.
BUT THEY'RE TOO BUSY PRAYING,
ASKING FOR HELP."

"GOD IS NOT GOING
TO GIVE US ANYTHING MORE
UNTIL WE BECOME GRATEFUL
FOR WHAT WE HAVE."

Eppley Chemical Dependence Treatment Center (which has closed due to managed care and insurance issues) had an extensive one-year training program. The counselors at The ARCH Halfway House suggested I go into the training program. I wanted to, but it was a full 46 hours a week commitment with no pay. I was paying child support, happily I might add, and couldn't afford to not work full time.

One day a newspaper ran a story about a Tough Man Contest with a $5,000 first prize. I thought, "That's it. God's going to let me take my crazy past and turn it into an asset." I entered, but had only six weeks to get into shape. About that time, the movie "Rocky" had just come out and I began running the streets, shadow boxing. People on porches were hollering, "Rocky!" as I ran by.

I hurt my bad knee running up and down hills. One week before the first night of fights I couldn't even walk, and thought I'd have to drop out. I was really bummed. While doing my night meditation, I opened the Bible randomly. There in Psalms I read a passage which said, "He teaches my feet to be like hind's feet and my hands to war." I was excited because I thought it was a message from God to fight. Hallelujah!

My brother, Steve, came down to be my second or corner man. Steve brought a big heavy duty knee brace, which I put on over my smaller one. It kept my leg from bending, but I couldn't put any weight on it. I was very limited and ended up tied for fifth place. I did quit smoking for my training and haven't ever smoked since, so I actually won quite a lot, but no money. It was a lifesaver though, because it made me feel good to be able to fight a little bit. All 32 of us guys in the tournament were telling each other, "Yeah, you're tough, man." It was also probably good I didn't win the tournament, because it might have been too much for my false pride and triggered my addiction.

My friends kept pushing me to take the first step and sign up for the Eppley training. If that was God's will, He would show me the way, they said. The first part of training was to go back through treatment at Eppley for one month. I talked to my boss and he said he'd let me work evenings after one month of treatment. Since I couldn't afford not to work, because of my child support payments, I thought I'd write the Hall County Attorney, tell him what I'm doing, and seek financial help to pay that month's child support. I was notorious in Hall County and thought everyone would be happy I was trying to improve myself and sparing them the misery of all my criminal activity.

The county attorney was happy I was getting better. He wrote me to say how proud everyone was of me, but that they didn't have any money to pay my child support payment for a month. He wrote, "I checked the books and you are one month ahead in your child support payments, so you don't have to worry about this month."

"No way," I thought. I didn't make enough money in one 15-day paycheck to pay my child support. I had to send my payment in twice a month from both paychecks. There is no way I was ahead a month in my payments. I've always felt that God made that month's payment. I believe that even more so as my life has unfolded.

In treatment, I had some difficulty with grief over missing my kids and my wife. At this time, an old, unkempt, angry black man came into treatment. He alienated himself from all the patients due to his anger. That day I put out the effort to reach out to him. That night, to my surprise, he came into my room. He realized somehow that I was having problems and said, "You know, Bill, people pray to God Almighty asking for His help and He helps them, but they're too busy praying to God Almighty asking for His help."

I thought, "What is this old guy saying?" At first, I thought he was just crazy, and I was amazed that he had come into my room....and how did he know my name?

But then, I realized he was telling me something very important, very insightful. God Almighty does answer our prayers, but we're too anxious or busy to acknowledge our answered prayers because we're asking for more.

I truly believe God is not going to give us anything more until we become grateful for what we have. Gratitude is the answer and the best gift we can give back to God.

**"WHAT
YOU ARE
IS GOD'S GIFT
TO YOU.**

**WHAT YOU MAKE
OF YOURSELF
IS YOUR GIFT
TO GOD."**

The next morning when I woke up, that old, unkempt, angry black man had gone. He had walked out of treatment that night. He had been there less than 24 hours. I believe with all my heart that he was an angel who came and delivered a message to me and then left. If I hadn't reached out to him in kindness and love, I would have missed the message. Here it is 28 years later and I haven't forgotten what he had to teach me.

Five months into the 12-month training program, I began to realize how easily I could accidentally mentally, psychologically and spiritually hurt a patient. I understood this from personal experience. When I was in training, most of the counselors didn't have college educations. Their experience and qualifications were from their own recovery experiences. They were well-meaning, but sometimes brutal in their confrontations and/or communications skills.

I became sober from all the help I received in treatment at the ARCH and in counselor training, so treatment worked. However, it took a couple of years into my recovery to heal from the emotional scars I experienced from the brutal confrontation style of some counselors. When I became aware of emotional injuries and scars caused by the ways I had been confronted and emotionally beaten down, I became concerned.

I remember clearly saying to God, "God, I don't want to cause any more pain in anyone's life. I've caused all the pain I ever want to cause in people's lives. Maybe I'm not ready to be a counselor yet. Lord, if You want me to continue in this training program, You're going to have to let me know. Unless you somehow tell me that You won't let me hurt anyone, even if I'm messed up, you'll make sure I won't hurt my clients, otherwise I'm going to drop out." At this same time, I was working 46 hours a week for free in the training program, working 40 hours a week in my evening job and getting my room and board free for helping out at The ARCH.

I was reading a book on psychological disorders while studying in the training program when all of a sudden the words "Nervous Breakdown" just illuminated for me. I realized I was about to have a breakdown from working so many hours and only getting three or four hours of sleep a night. I realized I had to quit the training program or my job. I only had enough money to last three weeks without a job. I talked to my boss, Pete, and told him I needed to quit my job and just rest until my money ran out. Pete assured me that he would hold off filling my position for a month, in case I needed to come back to work.

Then another "Miracle" happened. Without having talked to anyone at Eppley, the Director called me into talk with him. He said, "Bill, you've been doing a wonderful job. You've proven yourself to be one of our best counselors and we don't want to lose you. We have a counselor position open in our new adolescent program that we are going to develop. I would like to hire you and at the same time you'll continue in our training program." At the time I was only in the sixth month of a year-long program. They had never hired anyone early before.

It was very clear to me that God wanted me to be a counselor and had given me His word to never let me harm anyone. I trust that God is continuing to keep His word and not allowing me to cause any harm.

I became a big advocate to change the abusive confrontational style to a gentler, loving, non-shaming technique. Back then, there was an ongoing conflict between the new discipline of chemical dependence counselors and mental health professionals. The chemical dependence counselors were recovering alcoholics and didn't like it if you had degrees. As alcohol and drug counselors became more educated, the profession has changed drastically. We're able to break through the denial of addictions in a much more productive manner. Most C.D. counselors now have degrees and the profession has extremely good workshops and in-services to continually learn how to be more therapeutic.

CHAPTER 16

MASTER KEY TO RICHES

> **EMERSON:**
> **"DO THE THING**
> **AND**
> **YOU WILL HAVE**
> **THE POWER."**

> **"THE SECRET IS NOT TO ACCEPT**
> **FAILURE AS AN OUTCOME."**
>
> -Bob Vanderheiden-

I read a book entitled "Master Key to Riches" by Napoleon Hill and was so affected by it that I'm going to devote a chapter to it. I also suggest everyone buy a copy of his book. According to Hill, there is only one sure way to the riches of life and that is through the philosophy of the Master Key to Riches.

The Master Key to Riches provides a way to complete possession of our own minds and thus control over our emotions. But to do this, the soil must be readied.

There are at least two selves, one is negative and the other is positive. We operate out of one or the other at all times and like a magnet draw either the positives or negatives out of all life experiences. This reminds me of the story that we all have two wolves in our nature: one is good, and one is bad. The question is, how do you control the wolves? Easy – don't feed the bad one.

For anything to be of lasting value, it must be shared and this is the greatest of all gifts because through giving we receive. Hill lists the Twelve Great Riches (pg. 1-12).

The Twelve Great Riches:

1. **The Positive Mental Attitude:** This is the starting point, it attracts, it is a state of mind
2. **Sound Physical Health:** This means thinking in terms of health and not in terms of illness.
3. **Harmony in Human Relationships:** Shakespeare said, "To thine own self be true, and it must follow, as the night the day, thou canst not then be false to any man."
4. **Freedom from Fear:** There are seven basic fears that men experience: fear of poverty, criticism, ill health, loss of love, loss of liberty, old age and death.
5. **The Hope of Achievement:** The greatest of all happiness comes with the hope of achievement of some yet attained desire.
6. **The Capacity for Faith:** Faith is the connecting link to infinite intelligence – a spiritual "chemical" that when mixed with prayer makes the connection.

7. **Willingness to Share One's Blessings**
8. **A Labor of Love**:   The highest form of human expression of desire.
9. **An Open Mind On All Subjects**: Tolerance is a true indication of intelligence.
10. **Self Discipline**: If man is not the master of himself, he cannot become master of anything. The highest expression of success is humility of heart.
11. **The Capacity to Understand People**: We must first understand ourselves if we are to understand others. All human activities are inspired by one or more of these nine basic motives of life-love, sex, material gain, self preservation, freedom of body and mind, self expression, life after death, anger and fear.
12. **Economic Security**: It is not attained by money alone but by the good service one renders. We must proceed with outstretched hands to give and to receive aid. To get one must first give.

These twelve principals are prerequisites for conditioning our minds to receive the Master Key to Riches. We operate from either a positive or negative (or both) outlook and if we are to grow up in our personal lives, it must begin with some amount regardless of how small of a positive mental attitude or at least the desire for it. I remember when I was desperate enough to try anything and became willing to try the 12-Step program.

I could see how back then my fear of getting old influenced my actions at times and I needed to confront that fear and all my fears in order to be free to experience life. Hope of achievement is the greatest form of all happiness. Just think about how important goals are in life – not so much the actual reaching as the working towards. A good example for me was the joy of going to college.

Sharing, love, and the capacity to understand are all so important to our very being – our need for people, everyone's need for each other. I have found that life just doesn't fulfill without it being a "we" journey – I believe we were made to need each other and to need God even though our self-wills keep getting in the way at times. None of this would be possible, except very selectively, without tolerance which for myself has been a painful process of learning. I believe tolerance is a true measure of education, knowledge, maturity, love, freedom and maybe one of the greatest gifts we can give ourselves and others. One of the greatest gifts I can give my loved ones is to allow them to have a bad day, without taking it personally.

These ideas are part of the process in preparing the soils of our minds to receive the good that life has to offer. Hill lists what he calls the Eight Princes for preparing our minds (pg. 13-19).

The Eight Princes:

Gratitude is the next step in the conditioning of our minds for the acceptance of riches. These gratitude topics are the real "conditioners" of our mind, the real builders of appositive mental attitude.

Napoleon Hill challenges us to follow his directions by remembering how people disbelieved Morse, Marconi, Edison and the Wright Brothers when they tried to announce their new ways. So he says that every night we are to have a round table session with these eight topics to express and thus reinforce our gratitude for their help each day.

1. **Material Prosperity**: I am grateful for
2. **Sound Physical Health**: I am grateful for:
3. **Peace of Mind**: I am grateful for:
4. **Hope**: I am grateful for:
5. **Faith**: I am grateful for:
6. **Love**: I am grateful for:
7. **Romance**: I am grateful for:
8. **Overall Wisdom**: I am grateful for:

It is the daily habit of gratitude for these topics that keep our minds fixed on what we desire and off what we don't desire. It's what keeps our minds focused on our major purpose in life and helps to keep the door closed on all negative thoughts.

Gratitude gives us the power to look for the equivalent good in all adversity and mastery over our most formidable adversary: ourselves. Observe that we ask for nothing, but devote the entire ceremony to an expression of gratitude for the riches that have already been bestowed upon us.

Exercises in gratitude are most helpful in developing a positive attitude. The plan is to fill our minds with positive thoughts so we don't have time to think about negatives. Making out gratitude lists is a very important part of my daily meditation and prayer. Many times it's in the form of a letter to God. In the beginning of sobriety, one of my favorite reminders was, "I don't have everything I want, but thank you God, I have everything I need."

Definiteness of Purpose:

There are seventeen principles of the Master Key to all riches. The Master Key is not any one of these principles, but the secret is in the combination of all the principles working together. Our preparation consists in the application of the first five of these principles and the first one is a "definite major purpose."

Singleness of purpose, having a definite major purpose, clear and concise, written out on paper and read out loud each day to keep it fresh in our minds is the idea of a definite major purpose. Hill said only two people out of a hundred have a definite clear idea of what they want and that is one reason why they never feel satisfied.

"Any idea that is held in the mind, emphasized, feared or reverenced, begins at once to clothe itself in the most convenient and appropriate physical form that is available." (p. 43) Ideas are the beginning point of a definite major purpose and whether it is only a passing thought or materializes into being has to do with if we act on it or not. If we decide on a definite goal and are willing to go for it, the ways to achieve that purpose will reveal themselves. Definiteness of purpose should completely occupy the mind so there is no room for thoughts of failure. My good friend, Bob, is an extremely successful businessman. He said, "The secret is not to accept failure as an outcome or possibility." He said, "Bill, I remember when you started college and no one expected you to stay with it, but you never had failure as a possibility and just stayed with it."

Hill believes a major weakness of most men is that they see the obstacles but don't realize the spiritual power than can help them overcome the difficulties. He feels one of the ways obstacles are overcome is by finding someone else with greater problems and helping them. This is a cornerstone of 12-Step programs. Through helping others and reaching out to them, we find the path ourselves. This works in all areas, especially in industry where harmony is very important and looking out for fellow workers can result in greater production.

"Singleness of purpose." It must be a burning desire and we must be willing to pay any price.

This idea helped me realize the importance of having a clear-cut idea of what I wanted out of life. Not just an abstract idea which I believe is what most people have, but something that can be written down, then action must be taken towards the achievement of the goal. Singleness of purpose is a strong thought that helps motivate us and keep us from procrastinating.

When I was seven years sober, I was given the opportunity to be the director of a new treatment center. I accepted, but soon felt overwhelmed, like it was totally all up to me for it to be a success. I remembered feeling that way when I began college and during my training at Eppley. None of it could have happened if I had not, with blind faith, taken steps toward my goal.

The Habit of Going the Extra Mile:

Definiteness of purpose and the habit of going the extra mile blend together to create a powerful force. They are but two of the seventeen principles that, when blended together, connect like links of a chain, creating a tremendously powerful force.

Going the extra mile must be done with a positive mental attitude and applying this principle creates a positive mental attitude. Some advantages of going the extra mile are it brings favorable attention to the individual, makes one indispensable, leads to mental growth and physical skill, protects against the loss of employment, and enables one to stand out because most people do not operate this way.

Going the extra mile gives a reason to ask for better pay because if we are only doing our pay's worth then we don't deserve to make more. It is a builder of sound character because it makes a person feel better about him or her self. It leads to harmony and understanding and sympathy for the weak and unfortunate.

It is a spiritual axiom that it is impossible to render extra service and not in some way be compensated for that extra effort. There are two forms of compensation to the man who works for wages. One is the wage and the other is the skill he attains from his work.

Going the extra mile without expecting any specific reward in return feels good. I feel good at work just doing the best job I can and not worrying about the pay, because I get paid in so many different ways, especially in a lot of love returned. As I learn more about people, I learn more about myself and as I learn more about myself I learn more about people.

Rather than being worried about being taken advantage of or if others are working hard enough and getting upset over it, I just do my best and it feels good. That can promote harmony and peace.

Remembering to go the extra mile can put some fun in life and put us in a position of advantage because of the law of return.

Love is the greatest experience of man. According to Hill, the emotions of love, sex and romance are the three sides of a powerful triangle of achievement. "Love is an outward expression of the spiritual nature of man" (p. 67).

This is a life-giving love that knows no selfishness, greed, jealousy or envy and makes the humblest of men a king. It is the foundation on which a true positive mental attitude can be maintained. The habit of going the extra mile develops this type of love by giving service to others unselfishly. Ralph Waldo Emerson said, "The magnanimous know very well that they who give time, or money, or shelter to a stranger – so it be done for love, and not for ostentation – do, as it were, put God under obligation to them, so perfect are the compensations of the universe. In some way, the time they seem to lose is redeemed, and the pains they take, remunerate themselves" (p. 68).

If a man knows what love is, he will love all mankind, the good and the bad, because he will understand that often times circumstances have helped to bring about the good or the bad qualities. Going the extra mile in the spirit of love must be done willingly and graciously and, if need be, the willingness to go a second or third extra mile may be necessary.

The greatest payoff of love and service is the friendships that endure. No man can experience enduring success except through the help and service of others.

Love and care are very important for successful living, but I believe the selfless love that Hill speaks of is definitely something that has to be developed through service to others. This requires at times much effort on my part, because sometimes I don't want to inconvenience myself. However, as Emerson said, we are repaid somehow through the spirituality of life and for me that payment has been a deep understanding and belief that God really is guiding me and that He has a wonderful plan for my life.

The Master Mind Principle:

"Definition: An alliance of two or more minds blended in a spirit of perfect harmony and cooperating for the attainment of a definite purpose" (p. 87).

The key to this power is "harmony" and it is necessary so we can benefit from the strengths and weaknesses of each other. When people work together harmoniously toward a definite purpose, they push each other and find themselves feeling less stress and thinking more clearly.

Important relationships that this principle can benefit are marriage (the most important Master Mind alliance), in religion, and in one's area of work. One example of a Master Mind alliance is our government, another is our American system of industry, and a football team is also an example. Power attained through harmony of effort!

In order to attain one's Definite Major Purpose, it must be backed up with a continuous effort and a very important part of that are the relationships we develop. It is very important to seek out people who are positive and have something – qualities of self, knowledge, education we can benefit from. I used to think if I liked someone we would be friends. Today, I recognize my tendency to like a lot of people who aren't good for me, so I pick my friends more carefully. I can love someone and care about them, but I don't have to be around them.

It's important to be aware of the people we come into contact with and realize we can learn from even the humblest of our contacts. Reading is also an important part of the Master Mind principle and our reading should be chosen thoughtfully. Some authors may become our friends through their writings.

Loyalty is a very important quality of this principle; it helps to promote confidence. It's a good idea to keep the purpose of our Master Mind alliances to ourselves and our positive support system so as to keep those who would be negative from sowing seeds of discouragement.

All successful ventures, it seems to me, have as a basis some form of a Master Mind alliance. This is an important concept to understand, and it has made all the difference in the world to me. My boss, myself, and the people who work under me all work together for the benefit of each other and for the common good. I've become aware just how easily I can be influenced by others and with this awareness I've chosen my close contacts more knowingly. The main idea is that we need each other to succeed in life and to this end we should put some definite effort into developing our Master Mind alliances.

Applied Faith:

To have faith a person must condition his mind. A positive mental attitude is the first requirement that is acquired through self-discipline. This is the discipline already mentioned, like going the extra mile, definiteness of purpose and developing a Master Mind alliance. Faith is guidance from within; it is that power that doesn't believe in "impossible." It denies despair and allows obstacles and hardships to be learning experiences to grow from and develop trust and faith.

For faith to develop, it must be based on a willingness to risk whatever the circumstances demand, but as Emerson said, "do the thing and you will have the power." That is faith. We are given two paths to take, either the path of fear or the path of faith, and our choice depends on our mental attitude.

Faith can heal the wounds of sorrow and disappointment when we realize that defeat is only temporary, and should be seen as a challenge for greater effort and greater faith. We need to be "persistent," and not let a day go by during which we don't do at least one thing toward the attainment of our Definite Major Purpose.

Twenty-eight years ago, my life was a complete, absolute wreck. Faith is the only thing that brought me to where I am today.

I totally believe in faith and the absolute necessity for it in my life. I truly believe the concept about doing the thing and you will be given the power. That is faith!

In both the group process and individual counseling, my main tool is faith. I just believe in the process, the dynamics of group, my skills and the overriding power of God – and it has never failed in the 28 years I've been a therapist.

The Law of Cosmic Habitforce:

"The law of cosmic habitforce is nature's method of giving fixation to all habits so that we may carry on automatically once they have been set into motion" (p. 41). Every person is where he is and doing what he is doing as a result of the habits established. Whenever any two minds contact each other, there is born a third mind patterned after the stronger of the two. Most successful people will admit their success began from a close association with someone with a positive mental attitude.

Man alone of all nature has been given the ability to change his fixed habits, because he has the ability to control his thinking. According to Hill, most successful people have had their beginning due to some tragedy or failure that helped to break up the established habits (the grip of Cosmic Habitforce) and allowed them to formulate new habits. These new habits, when carried on for a certain length of time, become permanently fixed into Cosmic Habitforce.

All the principles of the Master Key are part of what makes up Cosmic Habitforce. Hill lists seventeen principles in his book. The seventeen principles are:

(1) Habit of Going the Extra Mile
(2) Definiteness of Purpose
(3) The Master Mind
(4) Applied Faith
(5) Pleasing Personality
(6) Learning from Defeat
(7) Creative Vision
(8) Personal Initiative
(9) Accurate Thinking
(10) Self Discipline
(11) Concentration of Endeavor

(12)   Cooperation
(13)   Enthusiasm
(14)   Habit of Health
(15)   Budgeting Time and Money
(16)   Golden Rule Application
(17)   Cosmic Habitforce

If we form new habits through following all of these principles for a long enough time, the habits will be permanently established. This is a lot like the A.A. program when, due to a lot of pain, failure, and despair, the alcoholic becomes willing to try anything, and through the program of A.A. all his old habits change into new positive ones that have been proven to work.

I employ the ideas brought out in "The Master Key to Riches," book and I believe the combination of all these different principles is the key to success in life.

The main ideas I have established in my life are singleness of purpose, going the extra mile, the need for others as expressed by the Master Mind alliance, the belief and use of faith as the greatest of all powers and developing and cultivating an attitude of gratitude so that I am aware of the many, many gifts I've been given.

I'm healthy, physically, emotionally and spiritually, but it's still easy for me to take it all for granted. I can easily forget my many blessings, if I don't on a daily basis write out my gratitude lists. All of these ideas and exercises are so very important and helpful habits to establish.

CHAPTER 17

HOW TO MAKE A DECISION

"WAIT UNTIL THE TIME IS RIGHT. IT IS SELF-DEFEATING TO POSTPONE OR PROCRASTINATE; IT IS ALSO SELF-DEFEATING TO ACT TOO SOON, BEFORE THE TIME IS RIGHT.
SOMETIMES, WE PANIC AND TAKE ACTION OUT OF FEAR. SOMETIMES, WE TAKE UNTIMELY ACTION FOR REVENGE OR BECAUSE WE WANT TO PUNISH SOMEONE. WE ACT OR SPEAK TOO SOON AS A WAY TO CONTROL OR FORCE SOMEONE TO ACTION. SOMETIMES, WE TAKE ACTION TOO SOON TO RELIEVE FEELINGS OF DISCOMFORT OR ANXIETY ABOUT HOW A SITUATION WILL TURN OUT.
AN ACTION TAKEN TOO SOON CAN BE AS INEFFECTIVE AS ONE TAKEN TOO LATE. IT CAN BACKFIRE AND CAUSE MORE PROBLEMS THAN IT SOLVES. USUALLY, WHEN WE WAIT UNTIL THE TIME IS RIGHT – SOMETIMES ONLY A MATTER OF MINUTES OR HOURS – THE DISCOMFORT DISSOLVES, AND WE'RE EMPOWERED TO ACCOMPLISH WHAT WE NEED TO DO."
"Language of Letting Go" (November 12th)

In January, 1985, I was given the opportunity to go to Hastings, Nebraska to develop and start up a Treatment Center. It was an exciting offer, but I didn't know if I was ready and I was reluctant to leave the place I got sober, and where I had a good support system. It would mean moving close to where I used to live and partied.

I talked and prayed about it, but was not able to make up my mind. I decided to drive the 300 miles home to see my parents and family in North Platte. I'd use that time on the highway to make a decision. As I drove, I realized the same repetitive thoughts kept going round and round in my mind: my morning meditation reading in the Big Book had said something about making a decision.

I pulled off the Interstate and read on page 86 of the Big Book:

> **"In thinking about our day, we may face indecision. We may not be able to determine which course to take. Here we ask God for inspiration, an intuitive thought or a decision. We relax and take it easy. We don't struggle. We are often surprised how the right answers come after we have tried this for awhile."**

I had read this paragraph hundreds of times, mostly just to get to the next paragraph, but had never really paid any attention to it. It never made sense to me and it really didn't that time either, but I was desperate. I had already done all the talking and writing out lists with pro's and con's I could try, so I decided to start driving, crank the music up and start singing loud. When I started to think,

I'd just sing louder to keep from thinking and just let go of the thoughts.

By the time I had driven 60 miles, I'd made my decision. I didn't really even have to make it. I just knew. Of course, I spent the next week second guessing if that was really God helping me or not. At an A.A. meeting, a woman said, "I've been praying for God's will, and I felt like God gave me direction, but I've been second guessing myself for six months until I finally took action."

I started laughing. That's what I had been doing. So I informed the Executive Director of Eppley that I was honored and excited to go.

This was an incredible miracle for me to be able to go back to where I had influenced so many people to use drugs and, instead, to help people get into recovery.

That simple paragraph from the Big Book gave me the formula to be able to make decisions and it has never failed. As I mentioned, every time I've applied it, I always felt like I didn't even make a decision. I just became aware of it.

My son, Dan, shared a Bible verse with me that has also been very helpful when I've felt confused.

"TRUST IN THE LORD WITH ALL YOUR HEART, AND DO NOT RELY ON YOUR OWN INSIGHT. IN ALL YOUR WAYS ACKNOWLEDGE HIM, AND HE WILL MAKE STRAIGHT YOUR PATHS."

(Proverbs 3:5-6)

CHAPTER 18

MARY LANNING EPPLEY TREATMENT CENTER SAINT THERESE

Mary Lanning/Eppley
Treatment Center

715 N. St. Joseph
Hastings, NE 68901
402/463-7575

> **"ST. THERESE WANTED
> TO KNOW IF I
> WANTED HER TO BE A PARTNER
> WITH ME IN
> THE TREATMENT CENTER
> I WAS STARTING.
> I WOKE UP SAYING,
> 'WHY, YES!
> OF COURSE I WANT YOU
> TO BE MY PARTNER.
> YES, YES, THAT WOULD BE GREAT,
> WONDERFUL!'"**

Life was good. I was on top of my profession. I not only was the director, but I was given the opportunity to develop the new center, from remodeling a hospital floor to hiring and training all the staff. I was in the newspaper, on radio, on television shows, and out giving talks and lectures. I was also engaged and in love. Everything had fallen into place.

A newspaper story ran in a special section on the front page of the Grand Island Daily Independent on January 4, 1988. The section titled "Extra/ordinary People," is only included in the newspaper a couple of times a year, and this time it was about me. The article read as follows:

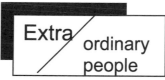

Former bad boy turns life around, now helping others

Nov. 22nd, 1978. That's the date Bill K. made a new beginning. It's the day he ended 20 years of heavy drinking and using drugs.

It's the date he became sober and he has stayed that way for more than 9 years.

It may not have been New Year's, but it was a day Bill made a resolution that he has kept.

Actually, what Bill made was a transformation. He has gone from being an alcoholic and a drug addict to counseling alcoholics and addicts.

Bill, who grew up in Grand Island, is director of the Eppley Treatment Center for drug and alcohol abuse at Mary Lanning Hospital in Hastings.

For those who knew him when he attended high school in Grand Island in the early 1960's, or for those who knew him before 1978, that may seem like an odd job for Bill.

As Bill Clinch, a counselor at the Eppley Center, said, Bill has gone 'from the bottom to the top.' Since he was 14 years old, Bill had been a heavy drinker, a drug addict and a fighter.

That was before Nov. 22, 1978.

'He was 180 degrees different from how he is now.' Said Dick Stalker, director of the Family Recovery Center.

'He was an angry man. He had a lot of resentment directed toward anybody who got in his way,' Stalker said.

Bill's anger came from his alcoholism and drug addiction.

Bill said he started to drink when he was 14 because he found 'it helped me dance better.' Once a promising football player, through drinking Bill lost his motivation and became violent.

Finally, during his senior year in 1962, he was kicked out of school for fighting.

'I didn't realize I had an alcohol problem,' he said. 'I just liked to party and have a good time.'

Bill then got married and joined the Navy where he learned to drink even more. And he kept fighting.

After getting out of the Navy, Bill moved to California where he started taking drugs along with his drinking.

He moved back to Nebraska and was working as a bouncer at a night club when he got shot in the stomach. During the trial of the man who shot him, the defense attorney tried to prove the man had shot in self defense because Bill's body was a 'lethal weapon.'

It was a reputation that Bill, 6 feet tall, 220 pounds and muscular, had deserved. 'I was in hundreds of fights,' Bill said. 'I once counted that I was in 350 fights. I must have put 100 people in the hospital.'

After being shot, Bill thought about changing his lifestyle and thought going to college would help and started attending Kearney State College. Although he graduated, it was there that he became even more involved in drugs. He was the leader of a drug ring, selling drugs and stealing. And his own addictions grew worse.

'Cocaine became my drug of choice,' he said. 'And I did

methamphetamines for years, staying up for days at a time, and also smoked pot daily.'

'Drugs and alcohol became more important to me than anything else. I was shooting up something every day.'

"I'VE NEVER SEEN ANYONE IN WORSE SHAPE THAN ME."

That included being more important than his wife and five children. Bill became so paranoid that he nailed shut all the windows and doors on his home in Grand Island. It was at this time his wife, parents and his in-laws confronted him with his problems. 'They put his life in front of him' said his daughter, Debbie Halm of St. Paul. 'It made him cry. It was very emotional, but he has been straight since.'

But getting straight wasn't easy. Bill first was treated for his addictions at the Veteran's Treatment Center in Omaha. He then spent a year and a half in a halfway house. It was during that time that he developed a faith in God.

'My first night in treatment I prayed, 'God if you're really there, if you really care, I'm willing to do whatever it takes,'

Bill said. 'All through my recovery, God has been my force and power. I couldn't do it by myself.

'When you're in treatment you learn a lot about yourself. You learn how to reach out to others and to let them reach out to you.

After his time in the halfway house, Bill entered a one-year training program at Eppley to become a counselor. He then worked at the Eppley Treatment Center in Omaha for several years. For most of that time he worked with young people.

'It was a real beautiful experience. Working with kids helped me to see the kid in everybody,' he said. 'It helped me get by the sickness. It's easy to get caught in the sickness and not see the person who is hurting, who needs love.'

As Bill sees it, he is now using for good the characteristics that made him a leader of the drug ring.

'It's like I have an asset, that I can develop a good rapport with people and they look up to me,' he said. 'Before, I was bad, steering people in the wrong direction. Now it's an asset I'm using to steer people in the right direction.'

'It has been hard though,' Bill added. 'My whole lifestyle has needed to change.'

For him and for anyone being treated for an addiction, Bill said one of the major steps was learning to trust the ones helping him through the treatment. For him, it also involved developing a trust in God. 'I have a lot of faith,' he said. 'God has brought me up from a complete wreck to where I feel good about myself. I'm proud of what I've done with my life.'

Bill, 43, said it has been enjoyable for him to move back to the Grand Island area. He has been the director of the Eppley Treatment Center in Hastings for two years. Bill said he has been able to help a lot of his old friends, people who once used drugs and drank with him.

For them, Bill's story has been encouraging.

'He is a man who really experienced an awakening...that he has a purpose in life,' Stalker said. 'He's one of the reasons I'm in this business. He has helped me and he will help a lot of people.'

Through the time he was drinking and taking drugs, Bill's marriage fell apart and he was divorced. His daughter, Halm, said his five children are just now starting to get closer to their dad.

'It was really a weight taken off when he got straight,' she said. 'It has taken awhile for us kids to get back on the right track. I'm just glad he has gotten his life together.'

There are other people who feel the same way. At Bill's 25th high school reunion this year, his classmates presented him with a certificate 'to the person whose life had most improved.'

That a person's life can improve is a message Bill now shares with others.

'No matter how bad it gets, it can get better,' he says from experience. 'I've never seen anyone in worse shape than me.'

Bill said before he got help he was bound to 'either be locked up for killing someone or else I'd be killed.'

He added that it's amazing how many of his friends are dead from overdoses, car accidents or suicide.

He doesn't want to see that happen to anyone else. 'I tell people that if life is really difficult there is help,' Bill said. 'There is an answer, there is hope no matter how hopeless it looks. All they need to do is give us a call.' And he knows what he is talking about.

My fiancé lived in Omaha, and on the day she and her bridesmaid went shopping for her wedding dress, they got high smoking pot. She never did get back into recovery and dropped me for the wild life. I had to back off too, because my recovery was in jeopardy. I was depressed and far from my support group in Omaha, my A.A. meetings, my recovery friends, and my sponsor. I did get a new A.A. sponsor in Hastings, but we really hadn't talked much.

At the hospital, a nurse was assigned to help me. She was Catholic and part of a perpetual adoration hour at church; someone was there every hour. Her hour was 2:00 a.m. to 3:00 a.m. One day she mentioned she was going to be out of town and asked if I was interested in taking her hour that night. I thought, I'm miserable, the church seems like a safe place and I can't sleep anyway. So I agreed.

I was despondent and brought my St. Jude prayer card to cling to while sitting in church at 2:00 a.m. St. Jude is the patron saint for hopeless cases, and I felt pretty hopeless. I looked for something to read, but whoever had cleaned the church that evening locked everything up. There was absolutely nothing to read. Not even a Bible was left out. But on a long shelf, I found a simple prayer card about St. Therese.

I'd heard about a St. Therese who supposedly would send roses to let you know God was hearing your prayers and on the prayer card she says, "I will let fall from Heaven a Shower of Roses." I didn't believe in that hocus pocus bullshit though. When the hour was over, I went back to my house and fell into a restless sleep.

The next day, I returned to my desk after an errand and found a rose sitting on my desk. The accompanying card was unsigned and read, "I just thought someone should send you a rose." I couldn't believe it.

Later, I went over to see my new sponsor, Joe, and told him the story. He became very excited. "Bill, this is great! It's God telling you He's with you in your pain. He's watching over you." Joe also explained that St. Therese had been his family's patron saint for generations. It turns out Joe and his very large family (11 children) are very devout Catholics.

Joe liked to share that he had studied in the seminary to be a priest. "My 11 children are glad I dropped out, my two wives wish I would have stayed," he joked. Joe was a wonderful sponsor and taught me so much.

Well, I tried to get some solace from the card and the rose because I was desperate. The following night, I surprisingly went to sleep right away (which was unusual) and I had a vision. I'd never had one before and I've never had one since.

I dreamed I was sitting at my desk at the hospital and the St. Therese card was floating in the air at eye level. No strings, no cobwebs -- the card just floated there. I thought, "What the hell, how can that be?" Then this piece of white floated out of it and became a full-sized blank sheet of typewritten paper and it was floating too. I thought, "What in the world?" As I watched, the paper filled with typed words. I didn't have to read it, I knew what it said. It was a typed contract from St. Therese and she wanted to know if I wanted her to be a partner with me in the treatment center I was starting. I woke up saying, "Why, yes! Of course I want you to be my partner. Yes, yes, that would be great, wonderful!"

I woke up awed by what I'd seen in my vision. The next day I went to the Crossier Monastery and bought a couple of books about St. Therese to find out about her and who she was. It turns out St. Therese is, for Catholics, the patron saint for missions and missionaries! And that was exactly the type of treatment center I wanted and have continued to develop over the years. It is a mission, and I totally believe we are missionaries, trying to save lives.

I had a picture taken of the rose in its vase and the card next to it. I had this picture blown up to poster size and every treatment center I've started up has that picture hanging on the wall. St. Therese is my partner and the three treatment centers I've been fortunate to start up have all been incredibly successful. I'm blessed to have experienced so many people getting into recovery and living such wonderful lives.

Over the years, St. Therese has kept her word and sent me a shower of roses from heaven to let me know that God loves me and is guiding me.

ST. THERESE
OF THE CHILD JESUS

MY NOVENA ROSE PRAYER

O Little Therese of the Child Jesus, please pick for me a rose from the heavenly gardens and send it to me as a message of love.

O Little Flower of Jesus, ask God today to grant the favors I now place with confidence in your hands . . . .

(Mention specific requests)

St. Therese, help me to always believe as you did, in God's great love for me, so that I might imitate your "Little Way" each day.

Amen.

SOCIETY OF THE LITTLE FLOWER
1313 FRONTAGE RD. • DARIEN, IL 60561
1-800-621-2806
www.littleflower.org

J3541

ST. THERESE, THE LITTLE FLOWER

Therese Martin was born to Louis Martin and Zelie Guerin on January 2, 1873. At the age of 15, she entered the Carmelite convent at Lisieux, France. With the religious name of St. Therese of the Child Jesus and the Holy Face, she lived a hidden life of prayer. She was gifted with great intimacy with God. Through sickness and darkness, she remained faithful, rooted in God's powerful love. She died on September 30, 1897, at the age of 24.

The world came to know her through her autobiography, "The Story of A Soul." She described her life as "a little way of spiritual childhood." She lived each day with unshakable confidence in God's love. What matters in life is "not great deeds, but great love."

The inspiration of her life and her powerful presence from heaven touched so many people so quickly that she was solemnly canonized on May 17, 1925 by Pope Pius XI. Had she lived, she would have only been 52 years old at the time of her canonization. In 1997, St. Therese was declared a Doctor of the Church by Pope John Paul II.

"My mission — to make God loved — will begin after my death," she said. "I will spend my heaven doing good on earth. I will let fall a shower of roses." Countless lives have been touched by her intercession, and millions have imitated her "little way." She has been acclaimed the "greatest saint of modern times." Everywhere in the world, her roses continue to fall.

- The portrait of St. Therese (cover) by her sister Celine, is considered the most authentic representation of the Saint ever done. The original is at the National Shrine of St. Therese in Darien, Illinois.

MIRACULOUS INVOCATION TO ST. THERESE

O Glorious St. Therese, whom Almighty God has raised up to aid and inspire the human family, I implore your Miraculous Intercession. You are so powerful in obtaining every need of body and spirit from the Heart of God. Holy Mother Church proclaims you "Prodigy of Miracles... the Greatest Saint of Modern Times." Now I fervently beseech you to answer my petition *(mention here)* and to carry out your promises of *spending Heaven doing good upon earth... of letting fall from Heaven a Shower of Roses*. Little Flower, give me your childlike faith, to see the Face of God in the people and experiences of my life, and to love God with full confidence. St. Therese, my Carmelite Sister, I will fulfill your plea "to be made known everywhere" and I will continue to lead others to Jesus through you.

Amen.

"I will let fall from Heaven ...
a Shower of Roses" -ST. THERESE

CHAPTER 19

GOD BLESS MY FAMILY

"DAD SAID,
'BUTCH, I AM SO VERY PROUD OF
YOU AND I LOVE YOU. YOU'RE
NEVER ALONE.
I'M WITH YOU ALWAYS.
I AM WITH GOD AND
GOD LETS ME BE WITH YOU.
I'M ALWAYS HERE WITH YOU.'"

I am so very fortunate to have the wonderful families I have. I have many families: my birth family, which consists of my parents, grandparents, nine siblings, about 35 nieces and nephews, my five wonderful children, 15 wonderful grandchildren, cousins, aunts and uncles.

My many, many wonderful friends, old and new, are also part of my family, as are my 12-step support family and my work family. I am so blessed to work with my best friends as co-workers. Others in my family are:

- Jesus – God the Father, Son and Holy Spirit
- My Church
- St. Therese, St. Joseph, St. Jude, Mary, St. Anthony
- My horse, Cutter, cat, Kisses, and dog, Coal

The truth is I'm a big baby and need a lot of love. I know that. Fortunately, I've always had a lot of friends. Unfortunately, until I got sober, I wasn't able to be a good, positive friend. I was a terribly bad, negative influence on my friends, but I thought I was a good friend. One of my best friends sold drugs for me; I'd trained him how to do it. Bob eventually disappeared with a large quantity of crystal meth of mine and I found out he had checked himself into Hastings Regional Center. I didn't realize it was a treatment center for alcohol and drugs. I didn't know there were treatment centers. I thought he was in a nut ward and I went and found him. I made him come out to my car and ride around to smoke a joint and tell me what his problems were. He did convince me he wanted to stay, so I let him. I'm sad to say that later he was killed in a car accident, drunk. I just didn't know back then that we all had a disease called chemical dependence.

When I first went to treatment, my wife divorced me and my kids were very confused because their mom didn't want me around them. I felt total grief, loneliness and despair. The guys at ARCH and my sponsors told me I needed to replace that loss with the guys around me. I know now this is called people replacement. I didn't want them, I wanted my wife! I wanted my kids!

The guys hung in with me and forced me to go to movies, dances, etc. They loved me and cared for me long before I was able to love or care for myself.

One of the most important ingredients a treatment center or halfway house needs in order to be successful is a family atmosphere. It has to generate a feeling of love and understanding, and the knowledge that everyone's success is dependent on each other.

You're needed! You need them! We became family, and not just for the moment, but for life. I have so many wonderful friends all around the country. I may not see them for a year, maybe I'll never see them again, but they'll always be in my heart and I'm in theirs.

My friend, Susie, says at any given moment we are making wonderful memories.

Like I had already mentioned, God made us to need Him and to need each other. We can't be happy until we recognize and allow these needs to be fulfilled.

My father died September 11th, 1998, and my mom and all of us miss him very much. I was in therapy doing what is called Eye Movement Desensitization Reprocessing (EMDR) with my therapist. I purposely chose him because he had that skill. During a session I had a conversation with dad. I was working on anger, fear, and grief at the time. I was crying and feeling alone when dad said to me, "Butch", his nickname for me, "I am so very proud of you and I love you. I know you realize how tough your mother and I brought you up to be physically, but we also brought you up to be strong mentally and that's why you're able to do the work you're doing. You're never alone. I'm with you always. I am with God and God lets me be with you. I'm always here with you." It made me cry then and it's making me cry now, but it's so wonderful. I haven't felt deep loneliness since then.

I always thought I needed to fill up that lonely hole in my soul with God. That day I learned I needed to fill it up with God and dad.

I always understood how important mothers are for the nurturing love they give, but until that day I never realized how important fathers are for providing a sense of security and safety.

Mom and dad are still teaching this 62-year old guy. Funny, back when I was 17, I thought I knew everything already.

The one clear point I hope to emphasize, and re-emphasize, is the only thing strong enough to overcome addictions or any problem is the power of love. I think God is love. Sometimes He works alone, but most of the time He works through people. Sometimes we are the angels He works through.

EMDR therapy was so helpful that I became certified myself. I have watched many clients get in touch with and work through traumatic experiences.

Once more I want to express how extremely important my family is to me. My mother, Shirley, and my father, Bill Sr., really dedicated their lives to bringing up all of us kids.

My oldest son, Gary, has all the same degrees I have and 14 years of sobriety. I want to share that on 8-15-05, Gary was also honored by being the featured person in the "Extra-Ordinary Person" column of the same newspaper I was featured in. That was very special! I think we're the only father and son who both were featured in this special feature. Gary has his own counseling agency called Keck's Counseling.

My daughter, Deb, and I don't have contact at this time. My son, Danny, is a very good man, a wonderful son and the kind of father I wish I could have been for him. My daughter, Kim, and her family have just come back into my life, and I am so happy. I need to say one of the proudest moments in my life was when I was given the honor of walking Kim down the aisle and giving her away on her wedding day. My youngest daughter, Billie, and her family are living with me at this time, which is a gift for us all.

I also want to share that I had a wonderful gift in a past relationship. I was allowed to be a father figure for a little Chinese girl named Molly when she was between the ages of 1 to 7. I was sober, so I was able to experience the joy of helping her take her first steps, her first day of school and all the other joys that can truly be enjoyed when sober. Molly and I were a gift to each other and, although I haven't been allowed to have contact with her for the past seven years, she'll always be my little girl too. So really I have six children, counting little Molly, and I hope someday to be reunited. But that, like everything else, is in God's hands.

CHAPTER 20

MENTAL BREAKDOWN

**"IF I WAS
LUCKY ENOUGH
TO GET BETTER,
I DIDN'T EVER, EVER
WANT TO
FORGET
HOW
DARK
IT
WAS."**

Prior to having a severe mental breakdown, I thought I knew what that was. I had no idea; I don't believe any one can comprehend what a breakdown is unless they experience it.

If you can imagine the most horror-filled moment you've ever experienced and felt like that every single second of every single minute, for every single hour of every day of every week for three months, you might have some insight to the horror I felt. It's so sad to think about how many, many human beings are stuck in that horror.

I believe a medical condition and the operation I had for it triggered my mental collapse. On Superbowl Sunday of 1988, the last day of January, I called my sponsor, Joe, and told him all I could think of was suicide. It was the only clear thought I had and it was as simple and clear as two plus two equals four. I was thinking about borrowing someone's gun. I thought I'd tell them I wanted to go hunting, but I looked so bad, no one would have believed that.

Joe took me to Richard Young Psychiatric Hospital in Kearney. I was in bad shape. I knew who I was, I knew my name, but I had no sense or feeling of myself. I called my friend, Art, in Florida and told him what happened. He couldn't believe it; nobody could because I had been bigger than life. Art said, "Bill, you're going to make it, you're strong."

I said, "Art, I don't know what that means. I have no sense of what being strong means." It had no meaning. Finally I said, "The only thing I know is that I trust you and if you say I'm strong, I'm going to try and believe you."

That's what I had to do. I was in a locked ward under suicide watch. In the morning, the exercise therapist would have us line up and try to do some exercises. I cannot begin to share how incredibly hard and difficult it was to make myself roll my head from side to side. In fact, the only way I could do this was to realize how important it was to the other poor patients to see me doing it. Trying to initiate action was almost beyond my capabilities.

I thought hard about getting out and walking in front of a train so it wouldn't look like suicide, and to spare my family that pain. Thank God for my Catholic upbringing, because it made a difference with the suicidal thoughts.

After about 20 days, I was walking across my room when, for a fraction of a second, I felt like myself. It was only a blink on the screen, but I thought maybe I was going to get better.

One of the therapists made a meditation tape for me to listen to. It was about walking through a meadow and rafting gently down a stream. It was about 20 minutes long. It was a life saver. I listened to it over and over and over and for the length of the tape, I could sometimes not feel so scared and horrified.

My boss was keeping my Director job open for me, but I couldn't get better. My parents and family came to see me. My youngest brother, Dick, and his wife, Kristy came every day to be with me. I could not sit still, so Dick would have to walk up and down the hallway with me hundreds of times. He brought a couple of dumbbells and would help push me to exercise with him. It was so hard! He was only about 18 years old at the time and was somewhat in shock that his oldest, biggest and toughest brother was a crying basket case. He would say, "Just take deep breaths, you're going to be okay. Just take deep breaths."

So many, many times over the years with hundreds of clients I've been able to help them slow down by saying, "Okay, you're going to be okay. Let's concentrate for just this moment on taking deep breaths. In order to slow your brain down and stop all the anxiety, we first have to slow your body down. So slow down, you're safe right at this moment, just take some deep breaths." It's amazing how well that works.

While in Richard Young Hospital, one day the occupational therapist had us make frosted mirror glass images. I decided to make a dove with a twig in its beak (a dove with a rose in its beak was the logo for the Eppley treatment center). I wrote the words, "IN THE DARKNESS" on it. If I was lucky enough to get better, I didn't ever, ever want to forget how dark it was.

My mom and dad came for a large (several families) group session once and, while I sobbed uncontrollably, my dad reached out and put his arm on my shoulder to let me know they were with me. How very wonderful, in that horror, to feel mom and dad's love.

Unfortunately, after 45 days, my insurance ran out and I wasn't any better. My boss sent me to Eppley treatment center in Beatrice where our best medical doctor was. It was depressing not to be getting better. It was a Friday evening when some A.A. guys drove about 600 miles altogether to get me to the hospital. I was so frightened I couldn't sit down. They called the doctor in that night and he talked to me, but I couldn't sit or lay down. Finally, after about two hours, I told him, "You are going to think I'm crazy, but I think maybe I can lie down if you promise to hold my hand and not let go. You have to promise to not let go until I say so." He said, "I promise to stay right here and hold your hand, even if I need to stay here all night."

That doctor, God bless him, held my hand for almost two full hours and talked to me until I finally told him I thought he could let go. I had to have a nurse sit with me right next to the bed all night. All the next two days, A.A. members came and stayed with me for one or two hours and God bless them, too, because they wouldn't leave until someone relieved them. The doctor had to spend about an hour with me the next night.

After three weeks, they realized they could not help me, but found a treatment center at a psychiatric hospital that thought they could. It was Gorski Relapse Prevention Center at Maplewood Hospital in Kokamo, Indiana. I was again devastated that I had to go somewhere else. I called my sponsor, Joe, and cried, "Joe, they want to send me to Kokamo, Indiana, to get help. Do you think this can be God's will for me?" Joe thought for a minute and said, "Bill, how else would a guy get to Kokamo, Indiana?" As sick as I was, I had to get a laugh out of that.

Earlier I mentioned how easily we counselors could accidentally hurt someone if we are not careful. I have an example of this to share. I was very blessed that everyone God placed in my life was extremely caring and gentle professionals. God knew I needed that gentleness and love.

However, in Beatrice we had a sex therapist that came to the center a couple days a week. It just happened that of the 12 patients in treatment, nine of them were female and right after I got there, the two males completed treatment. Of these nine women, six of them were gay. The sex therapist was a little rude and confrontational when one day, during a one-on-one session she asked me, "Are you gay?"

"What?" I said. "Why would you ask me that?" I'd never had anyone ever ask me that. "Of course I'm not gay," I stated.

She asked me, "Are you sure?" The way she questioned me was almost an accusation and I told her I thought she was out of line and I didn't want to talk to her anymore.

The problem was, my mind was stuck in repetitive thinking patterns. It's really insane when you have the same thoughts over and over and over for weeks, which had been going on for about two months prior to this incident. So guess what? I couldn't get this stupid thought out of my mind, this question, "Am I gay?" Writing about it now, I can't help but laugh, but at that time it was horrible. So, I flew out to Indianapolis, Indiana, and my new counselor, Dick Jeski, picked me up. It's about 1.5 hour car ride from Indianapolis Airport to Kokamo. As we were driving down the road, I said, "Dick, you're going to think I'm really strange or crazy and I really am, but I have to tell you something. This abusive sex therapist in Beatrice asked me, almost accused me, of being gay for no reason whatsoever and I'm not gay. But I can't get this stupid ass thought out of my head. Am I gay? That's all I keep thinking over and over, am I gay? That sounds pretty crazy, doesn't it?"

God bless Dick, he just sat there for a couple of minutes and then said, "What you're stuck in is what we call repetitive thinking syndrome, but we'll be able to help you with it, don't worry."

There were about 40 patients in treatment and they definitely thought this guy from Nebraska was pretty crazy. The patients finally would tell me, "Bill, will you knock off asking that stupid question? You're not gay!" And I'd respond, "Yeah, I know, but I keep thinking, am I gay?"

I finally had to look at that repetitive thinking like you would when you have a wood sliver in your hand that you can't get out. You just have to acknowledge that it's there and continue on. I'm happy to report that finally, once I started getting better, that crazy thought went away. It's funny now, but just look at how easily we can hurt someone if we're not healthy.

Finally, after being heavily medicated for a few weeks and going through the Relapse Treatment Program, I began to get better. I lost my Director's job, because I wasn't getting better and was feeling a lot of grief over it. One day, Dick Jeski said, "Bill, you need to change the way you are looking at this. I want you to say, "This is a small price to pay for finding myself." I wrote this down and read it many times a day. That change in thought perception helped, but there was still a lot of grief.

I flew back to Nebraska on May 5th. I was better!

I had talked Joe's daughter, Susie, and her husband into being foster parents for some of the adolescents that went through my treatment center. Little did I know that they would eventually be my foster parents. Susie was my best female friend, and asked me to come live with her family when I got back to Nebraska from treatment, and I did. I lived with this wonderful family for nine and one-half months before I was finally strong enough mentally to go back to work. I could never express how fantastic Susie and Dave Ryan and their children Sean and Carrie were to me. They truly loved me back to health and it was a very healing time.

God took one of my darkest times and turned it into one of the most memorable times. They were truly my family as much as my birth family. Today Susie and Dave have three more wonderful children, Joe and twins Kristie and Kevin.

I learned something incredible living with them, but I don't want to take anything away from my parents, who with every child became better and better parents. In my family we are very close and very loyal to each other. Mom and dad taught us about unconditional love. All that I am, all that I've been able to accomplish is because of what they taught me. I am so thankful and grateful to God for mom and dad.

When I moved in with the Ryans, we were comfortable from day one, yet something felt strange. One day I figured it out. In my family and the family I started, we all loved each other deeply, but the reason we behaved was because we didn't want to get punished. Little Sean and Carrie were very well behaved kids also, but the reason they behaved was because they loved and respected their parents' wishes. If they didn't behave right, they would of course have consequences, but that really wasn't the overriding factor.

If I hadn't had this horrendous experience, I would have missed my time with the Ryan's. I didn't know this mindset existed and I didn't know that I didn't know. Today I try to teach this new concept to my clients. Do what you need to do out of love and respect. Wow.

Don't get me wrong. My siblings all love and respect my parents very, very much. But somehow we never connected that with behaving correctly. Maybe, come to think of it, it was mostly the first three or four of us kids who didn't understand.

During the nine and one-half months I lived with the Ryan's, I was able to complete my Master's degree in Counseling and Guidance. This time I was really proud of myself and happy I could make my family and friends proud too.

A little history regarding starting my Master's degree. I had been sober for six years when all of a sudden at every A.A. meeting I went to someone was talking about going to college. I found myself feeling jealous, envious and frustrated, so I started praying about it. "Lord, please remove these character defects of envy, jealousy and anger from me." The more I prayed, the more I felt these shortcomings. Finally one day God revealed to me that it wasn't character defects, it was God telling me to get off my butt and get my Master's Degree. I also remember every time I ever went into the office of someone who had a M.S. degree plaque on the wall, it illuminated in my mind. I was supposed to get to graduate school.

I wrote my thesis about the trauma of a mental breakdown and how the mental health field, spirituality, chemical dependence field and Alcoholics Anonymous (A.A.) worked together through God's guidance to restore me back to wellness. This small book is titled, "In The Darkness."

Everyday I attended school, and if there was a rainstorm or a blizzard, all the better, I would stop in the middle of the campus and say, "Thank You, God." I never missed one day because I realized attending school was a gift. It was such a wonderful gift. My parents, siblings and children were there for my graduation and as proud for me as I was for myself.

I am living on borrowed time. I was dead twice and should have died many times, but for the Grace of God. It is so easy to get lost and miss out on the beauty of the moment. Today I just want to do God's will and enjoy the journey.

Several years after I graduated, a college friend stopped at my office to borrow money for a bus back to Kearney from Omaha. The last time I had seen him and his wife, they were doing great. He had his own business and was happy. When he came to see me, I didn't recognize him because he'd had a mental breakdown, lost everything, and was on disability. I was so sad for him, but also realized how blessed I was to have been restored to sanity, mental health. I wish my friend had been an alcoholic so he could have been slowly loved back to stable mental health like AA had done for me. My prayers are with him.

One of my favorite poems that has been very meaningful and helpful to me is titled, "Footprints":

FOOTPRINTS

One night a man had a dream. He dreamed he was walking along the beach with the LORD. Across the sky flashed scenes from his life. For each scene, he noticed two sets of footprints in the sand; one belonging to him, and the other to the LORD.

When the last scene of his life flashed before him, he looked back at the footprints in the sand. He noticed that many times along the path of his life, there was only one set of footprints. He also noticed that it happened at the very lowest and saddest times in his life.

This really bothered him and he questioned the LORD about it. "LORD you said that once I decided to follow you, you'd walk with me all the way. But I have noticed that during the most troublesome times in my life, there is only one set of footprints. I don't understand why when I needed you most you would leave me."

The LORD replied, "My precious, precious child. I love you and I would never leave you. During your times of trial and suffering, when you see only one set of footprints, it was then that I carried you."

-Ella H. Scharring-Hausen – 1922

CHAPTER 21

THANK GOD
BACK TO WORK

"FOR
UNTO
WHOMEVER
MUCH
IS GIVEN,
OF HIM
MUCH
SHALL BE
REQUIRED"
(Luke 12:48)

It took a couple of years back at work before I was mentally able to once again develop a treatment center.

An outpatient mental health clinic, "Operation Bridge," did good work with mental health, but at one time didn't believe alcoholism is a disease and tried to treat it as a mental illness. They didn't believe in 12-Step programs and consequently had little success working with chemically dependent clients. They were blackballed by the court system due to this problem, and sought me out to begin a 12-Step outpatient treatment program.

We had a very strong structured program that met four nights a week for 3.5 hours a night. We quickly became the largest outpatient 12-Step program in the State, having groups afternoons and evenings. It was an extensive treatment that also produced a high recovery rate, especially for outpatient treatment.

As part of this program, I also began working with the Siena/Francis Homeless Shelter in Omaha. I'd always planned on some day starting a treatment center for the many people who couldn't afford treatment. The executive director at the time, Paul Koch, kept trying to talk me into coming there, so we thought we'd try having me come in once a week and a couple of my counselors come in half-days.

We tried very hard, but it just didn't work. We couldn't get anyone to stay sober. Paul, God bless him, kept bugging me to come to work there full-time and I kept telling him, "I'd like to Paul, but I just can't afford to. I'd have to take a huge drop in pay, because I know you have a small budget." But he kept bugging me and I finally got kind of mad and said, "Paul, I've already told you I can't afford to, but just to make you happy, I'll do like I always do. I'll pray about it, ask for God's guidance, let it go and see what the answer is. I know what it'll be, but I'll do that this one time. Okay?" So I went to page 86 of the Big Book on how to reach a decision. It says:

> In thinking about our day, we may face indecision. We may not be able to determine which course to take. Here we ask God for inspiration, an intuitive thought or a decision. We relax and take it easy. We don't struggle. We are often

surprised how the right answers come after we have tried this for awhile.

What used to be the hunch or the occasional inspiration gradually becomes a working part of the mind. Being still inexperienced and having just made conscious contact with God, it is not probable that we are going to be inspired at all times. We might pay for this presumption in all sorts of absurd actions and ideas. Nevertheless, we find that our thinking will, as time passes, be more and more on the plane of inspiration. We come to rely upon it.

We usually conclude the period of mediation with a prayer that we be shown all through the day what our next step is to be, that we be given whatever we need to take care of such problems. We ask especially for freedom from self-will, and are careful to make no request for ourselves only. We may ask for ourselves, however, if others will be helped. We are careful never to pray for our own selfish ends. Many of us have wasted a lot of time doing that and it doesn't work. You can easily see why.

If circumstances warrant, we ask our wives or friends to join us in morning meditation. If we belong to a religious denomination which requires definite morning devotion, we attend to that also. If not members of religious bodies, we sometimes select and memorize a few set prayers which emphasize the principles we have been discussing. There are many helpful books also. Suggestions about these may be obtained from one's priest, minister, or rabbi. Be quick to see where religious people are right. Make use of what they offer.

As we go through the day we pause, when agitated or doubtful, and ask for the right thought or action. We constantly remind ourselves we are no longer running the show, humbly saying to ourselves many times each day, 'Thy will be done.' We are then in much less danger of excitement, fear, anger, worry, self-pity, or foolish decisions. We become much more efficient. We do not tire so easily, for we are not burning up energy foolishly as we did when we were trying to arrange life to suit ourselves.

It works – it really does. We alcoholics are undisciplined. So, we let God discipline us in the simple way we have just outlined.

I couldn't believe it!! The very next day, I knew I was supposed to resign, give my notice and go to work at the homeless shelter.

CHAPTER 22

SIENA/FRANCIS HOUSE

"I ALSO FELT GRATEFUL
THAT THIS POOR MAN
WAS AT A SAFE PLACE
AND FEELING LIKE
HE MATTERED.
HIS FOOD HAD
BEEN SERVED TO HIM
AND WE PRAYED OVER IT.
SOMETIMES
IT'S THE ONLY TIME
THEY FEEL SAFE."

It's very amazing how God works. As mentioned before, I had a dream to start up a treatment center for the desolate, poor and hopeless. A couple of my past patients were very wealthy and I was getting ready to lay some groundwork to get financial help asking for their ideas and support.

It wasn't until I started working at the Siena/Francis House that I realized this part of the dream was already in place. We already had the facility; we just needed to get the treatment program started. With all my previous experience developing treatment centers and programs, I thought this would be easy. Wrong!

The Siena/Francis House is the only "wet" shelter in all of Nebraska, meaning everyone is welcome, whether they are drunk or high. We take great pride in the fact that our doors are open to anyone. Our only requirements are they cannot bring alcohol, drugs or weapons onto the premises. If they cause trouble/violence or are caught with alcohol/drugs on the premises, we'll bar them for a specified amount of time.

This policy sounds disastrous to keep control, but it's really not. Many factors are at work: (1) the clients (homeless) know this is the last stop, so for the most part they try to behave; (2) Secondly, the shelter is run by the recovery program.

If not for the homeless shelter, we would not have a recovery program. If not for the recovery program, we would have a very small shelter. If not for both working together, thousands of our poor, sick, wounded and lost members of our country and community would not get the help they need.

We sleep around 400 people a night and serve over 800 meals a day. We distribute over 22 tons of clothing per year and it's all free.

Our Primary Mission Statement:

THE MISSION OF THE
SIENA/FRANCIS HOUSE IS
DIRECTED TOWARD A CONCERN
AND CARE OF THE POOR
FOLLOWING THE EXAMPLE OF
THE SCRIPTURES.

THIS MISSION IS REALIZED IN
FEEDING THE HUNGRY,
SHELTERING THE HOMELESS
AND CLOTHING THE NEEDY.
THIS MISSION EXTENDS BEYOND
MERELY ANSWERING PHYSICAL
NEEDS TO THE ACCEPTANCE
AND AFFIRMATION OF THE
HUMAN PERSON, THE CREATION
OF AN ATMOSPHERE OF
HOSPITALITY, AND THE
PROVISION OF PURPOSE AND
MEANING IN THE LIVES OF
PEOPLE WHO STRUGGLE FOR
SURVIVAL.

IT IS ALSO THE MISSION OF THE
SIENA/FRANCIS HOUSE TO CALL THE
GREATER OMAHA COMMUNITY TO A
SOCIAL CONSCIOUSNESS AND TO
ENLIST HELP AND SUPPORT IN THE
CARE OF THE HOMELESS
AND THE INDIGENT.

I'm hoping through this book to extend this "social awareness" to the world not just Omaha, Nebraska.

Sometimes I still experience deep feelings of fear and loneliness. I believe most of us have those feelings at times. The difference between me and a homeless person is I do have a safe home to go to. I have money to eat with, I have a job to go to. I have so much. I am healthy mentally and physically. I have a deep sense of spirituality. Most of the homeless population don't have these most basic necessities. They are extremely fearful and lost.

One day a man fell over dead while eating supper at the shelter. That was traumatic for everyone, myself included, but I also felt grateful that this poor man was at a safe place and feeling like he mattered when he died. His food had been brought to him and we prayed over it. For many of our guests, sometimes the only time they feel safe throughout the day is when they are sitting at the table being served.

What is even more important than food and shelter, I think, is to help them to feel some dignity, some sense of self-worth.

At any shelter, everyone has to keep close watch on their belongings or someone will steal it. Everyone knows that, but people on the outside don't realize there is an exception to this. I've watched this endless times: when someone is in very critical shape, physically or mentally, it's an unwritten code of ethics that you don't steal from them and you watch out for them. Of course, when they get better, all bets are off.

The death rate in the shelter is almost one person per month dying from the lifestyle. The average age of those who have died in the 12 years I've been there is late 30s to early 40s. It's heartbreaking.

The good news, the wonderful news, is we are making a difference! I can't speak for the country as a whole, but I can speak for Nebraska and especially Omaha and the surrounding areas about the generous donations of money, food, clothing and volunteer work.

I am very proud of all the support from our community and totally grateful to God for his wondrous plans. Shelters and treatment centers like ours are completely dependent on the goodwill of others, but it's a win/win situation for everyone. We wouldn't be able to do nearly as much as we accomplish if not for all the volunteers that help us. The win/win part is how much it helps our volunteers to feel good about themselves and a deeper sense of gratitude for their own blessings.

So if you want to help and feel better about yourself and life in general, just reach out to your local shelters and treatment centers in whatever way you're able. It's all part of God's plan in reaching out and helping others.

If you wonder what difference you can make, consider this story. One day a man was walking along the beach and in the distance he noticed a young man picking up starfish that had been washed up by the tide. As he watched, the young man began tossing the starfish back into the ocean. The man said, "Young man, why are you throwing those starfish back into the sea?" The young man replied, "The sun is up and the tide is going out. If I don't throw them back, they will die."

The man looked up and down the beach and said, "But there must be thousands of starfish washed up on the beach. How can you possibly make a difference?"

The young man bent down, picked up a starfish, threw it back into the ocean and replied with a smile, "I made a difference to that one."

Day House Program:

In 2005, Mike Saklar, Executive Director, and Rod Bauer, Day House Program Director, started and developed our Day House Program. This program has been wonderful. We've been able to help so many more homeless and needy people and get them the psychiatric and chemical dependency help they need. Rod came to the Siena/Frances "MIRACLES" Treatment Program in 1999 in extremely bad shape from methamphetamine, narcotics, etc., and has been sober ever since. He went back to college, earned two degrees and then received his Chemical Dependency Certification (LADC). We were able to hire Rod and now he has over seven years of sobriety.

A very dear card that Rod gave me back in 2000 reads:

Dear Bill – I'm glad you came into my life. You save people every day, but you saved me this time!! I hope some day I can be a vessel of God like you. I'm so very proud to be able to call you friend.

Love ya,
Rod

Of course we both know it's not myself or Rod, it's all just God working through us!

CHAPTER 23

"MIRACLES"
ADDICTIONS TREATMENT
RECOVERY PROGRAM

"PETE SAID,
'SISTER STEPHANIE, WE DON'T HAVE ENOUGH BLANKETS AS IT IS!'
SISTER STEPHANIE REPLIED,
'PETE, IF WE'RE SHORT OF BLANKETS OR ANYTHING, WE NEED TO GIVE AWAY WHAT WE HAVE SO GOD WILL SUPPLY US WITH MORE. YOU HAVE TO GIVE TO RECEIVE!'
(PHONE RINGS)
'HI, THIS IS THE HOSPITAL AND WE'RE REPLACING OUR BLANKETS. COULD YOU USE 150 BLANKETS?'"

A plaque I have at home and am making for my friends says:

> ## "WE DID NOT WALK
> ## INTO HIS LIGHT,
> ## HE
> ## CRASHED
> ## INTO OUR DARKNESS."
> ## THANK YOU GOD!

When I came to Siena/Francis, I thought I would just start the treatment center right up, using my past experiences. I was in for a big surprise. Everyday I came to work with plans written up to develop the program. Everyday, everything I set up would be shot down with all kinds of reasons why it wouldn't work. I got headaches daily from all the negative feedback about my plans. The headaches were due to the reality that their feedback was correct. I realized finally that this treatment center was going to require innovative and creative ideas for it to work.

All but a couple of men and women were using at the shelter and they kept it to themselves because not using was against the norm. Slowly, I weeded out the people using and kicked them out of the 42 beds designated for our recovery center. Everybody was really angry at me because I had upset the applecart. In order to kick people out, I had to catch them so they wouldn't feel like I was unfair and it was very important to not take away their dignity. This was a very difficult and slow process.

I tried to start group therapy about a month after I arrived, but I could not catch anybody to make them come. They purposefully eluded me and said they forgot. If I did physically catch them, they'd just come to the group room angry and pretend they were sleeping. It only took about two weeks of this fiasco to realize it was going to take a long time before I could have group therapy. So, I concentrated on one-on-one counseling with the few clients that truly wanted help.

My mom and dad came from North Platte, Nebraska to visit me and my new treatment center. After walking down the sidewalk with about a hundred drunk and high hardcore-looking individuals, many of whom had been to prisons many times with a lot of violence and anger in their lives, Dad stopped me on the walkway. He looked around and sincerely and quietly said, "I don't know, son, are you sure this is a very good or safe move for you?"

I smiled and said, "Oh yeah, dad, this is great. It's why I went through all that insanity I went through. So I can work with these people." Secretly, I was a little worried myself. In the evening, I would always put the window shades down, because I was afraid someone might machine gun my office. I had a beautiful gold 1979 Trans Am and I was afraid someone might blow it up.

There is a paragraph in the Big Book that I trusted for my safety and God's promise in the chapter, "Working with Others" (p. 102):

> **YOUR JOB NOW IS TO BE
> AT THE PLACE WHERE
> YOU MAY BE OF
> MAXIMUM HELPFULNESS
> TO OTHERS,
> SO NEVER HESITATE
> TO GO ANYWHERE
> IF YOU CAN BE HELPFUL.
> YOU SHOULD NOT
> HESITATE
> TO VISIT THE MOST
> SORDID SPOT ON EARTH
> ON SUCH AN ERRAND.
> KEEP ON
> THE FIRING LINE OF LIFE
> WITH THESE MOTIVES
> AND GOD WILL KEEP YOU
> UNHARMED.**

Isn't that a wonderful promise? I've experienced much solace and comfort from it. I give a lot of credit to Paul Koch for having the vision to pursue me so relentlessly to develop a recovery program. I also am very grateful for the faith he showed to allow total control to do what I thought best. Paul was a very good Executive Director and put his heart and soul into the Siena/Francis Shelter development.

We have two wings at Siena/ Francis for the "MIRACLES" program, one side for the women and one for the men, separated by a garden area. Fraternization is one of the biggest problems for any treatment center. Once an alcoholic/addict stops using a substance to make them feel better, the next best substance is the opposite sex (for some the same sex).

This is also a problem for all of us in 12-Step programs. We realize that when someone is a newcomer, they need to be given time to develop their recovery program. It's generally felt it's good to try to stay out of relationships for the first year. When someone with a year or more of sobriety tries to date a newcomer, it's referred to as, "hitting on a cripple." A big part of recovery is obtaining a sponsor and the sponsors help keep everyone in line. We all sponsor and have sponsors to keep ourselves in line. I can have the best intentions in all areas of my life, but still end up in left field if I don't check out my thinking. That is how we stay on track.

So stay away from sex that first year of sobriety, especially in a treatment center.

When I first started an actual group, we had 12 men and 7 women. It was exciting to finally have that many wanting recovery. At the beginning, the only role models the clients had in treatment were Sister Stephanie, Paul, Roc (Francis House Manager) and myself to give them hope or belief that they could get better.

Sister Stephanie was our spiritual director and an incredible example and teacher of faith. She was in charge of donations, which every shelter needs to meet the needs of the homeless. She has a wonderful philosophy that I'll relate in an actual story. It was winter and very cold out when a man came to the front desk and asked for a blanket to take to his homeless camp, but we didn't have enough for the guys in the shelter. Our front desk man said, "I'm sorry, but we don't have any extra blankets."

Stephanie heard this and said, "Pete, go ahead and give him a blanket."

Pete replied, "Sister Stephanie, we don't have enough blankets as it is!"

She answered, "It's okay, give him a blanket." Pete was upset, but gave the man a blanket. The man said, "I have a friend outside that needs a blanket also."

"Pete, give him another blanket," Sister Stephanie said. Afterwards, Pete complained to Sister Stephanie and she said her now famous quote:

> **"IF WE'RE SHORT OF ANYTHING,**
> **WE NEED TO GIVE AWAY**
> **WHAT WE HAVE.**
> **THEN GOD WILL SUPPLY US**
> **WITH MORE.**
> **YOU HAVE TO GIVE**
> **TO RECEIVE."**

Pete was arguing this belief when the phone rang. When he answered, the person on the other end said, "Hi, this is the hospital and we are replacing our blankets. We wondered if you could use 150 blankets."

This is what I believe and have seen happen over and over again. I want to thank my special friend, Sister Stephanie, for teaching me this law of God's universe.

If I went out the front door of the shelter and tried to convince the homeless, hopeless, desolate drunks, addicts and mentally ill into coming to treatment, it wouldn't work. I've tried it, especially at the beginning, and they won't listen. They can't hear me and don't believe it's possible. Do you know what they do hear loud and clear? What they see! When they see us give what we have materially from our hearts, that breaks through their defense mechanisms.

When they see someone who has lived on the streets get sober, have a real life, look happy, get a job and start families, they hear that loud and clear. This is how we have been able to be so successful and it all started with that first person.

I tell my clients all the time that for a family to get better, someone has to start. We help them to realize that someone is you, me.

I remember fondly that wonderful, amazing day the first person from our program got a "real" job. Our first graduate after nine months of being at the Siena/Francis House was hired by a local company. Then we had four, and then five people get jobs and graduate. Now, 12 years later, we have hundreds of graduates out there in the world.

We used to have many people come to treatment to get out of jail and they would end up being kicked out of treatment or would walk out. This has changed considerably due to our reputation that our clients have to work hard at looking at themselves. They are expected to change and get better. We won't accept anything less of them.

Most of our referrals call or write letters because they have been touched and motivated by our graduates or heard the message of hope from someone's family members.

We have people calling from all over the United States. So very many people need help and want help. When someone calls, they want to know what the requirements are. How much does it cost? I just love saying, "The only requirements we have are two questions: (1) Are you sincere about wanting help to stop using? and (2) Are you willing to make a commitment to follow all the rules and stay until you complete treatment? If the answer to both questions is, 'Yes,' that is all we require. There is no cost to come here, it's free, but you'll be expected to work very hard for the gift of being here."

MIRACLES Program Components: Basics Stage, PHASES I, II and III:

Basics Stage (30 days):

The Basics Stage allows a client to detoxify and allows time for the client to prove their sincerity and willingness to follow the rules.

- The client is on total restrictions from going off grounds, except with the rest of clients going on our bus/vans to 12-Step meetings.
- Client is assigned a counselor and completes Assessment/Evaluation Interview.
- First assignment is to read 164 pages in the Big Book and the "12-Steps Program Overview."
- They are assigned a 40-hour week job in the shelter.
- They are expected to obtain a sponsor during this time period and set up to attend meetings with their sponsor
- Begin attending group therapy/lectures Monday through Friday.
- Attend men's/women's group
- Participate in specialty groups such as Anger Management, Coping Skills, Dysfunctional Beliefs, Boundaries, Spirituality, Meditation, Big Book, 12x12, Grief, Men's Group, Women's Group, Communications groups, etc.

All these groups/lectures are important for the clients to begin working on themselves and to identify problems. This stage is very critical to set the tone for the client's recovery.

A very important tool is the Assessment/Evaluation Interview. This questionnaire was developed for four key functions:

1. To gain basic demographic information in all areas of client's life
2. To uncover any dishonesty and to break through client's denials (usually subconscious)
3. All of the questions are asked in at least two or three different ways so in the process the client learns more

about themselves and also disclose more than they had intended to. This automatically allows the therapist to gain a deeper level of trust quickly.

4. In the A.A. Big Book chapter "Working with Others," (p. 92), "Explain that many are doomed, it's an illness, a fatal malady. Doctors are rightly loathe to tell alcoholic patients the whole story of how hopeless the predicament. But you may talk to him about the hopelessness of alcoholism (addiction) because you offer a solution." When we put on paper the hopelessness of their lives and show that it's continuing to get worse, it can be a devastating insight. But that's good, because in order to get better, they must admit total defeat. That is Step 1. We do have a solution!

Our job training program is crucial to our success. It doesn't matter how sincere someone wants to look at themselves and character defects, they can only look so deep. All of us counselors spend a lot of the day in our offices with two or more clients who are having difficulty getting along for a myriad of reasons. These are the problems that would normally cause them to quit their jobs and go back to using.

It's a wonderful hands-on opportunity for coping skills development. This program helps them to develop the discipline necessary to get to work and to put in a 100% effort. All of the jobs have something to do with helping the homeless. It doesn't matter if it's working the front desk, working in the kitchen or maintenance, clean up or management. It's all necessary to help the homeless so the work makes the clients feel good. They have meaning, and feel worthwhile. They develop self-respect and a pride in self, which is a very necessary ingredient in recovery.

The clients have to attend minimum of five 12-Step meetings per week and three of those have to be outside meetings. They have to get a 12-Step sponsor. Getting connected to the various 12-Step programs and people is critical to ongoing sobriety.

"PHASE I" (minimum 90 days):
- Identify and develop treatment plan to work on problems
- Complete all 12-Step assignments
- Progress in job from SST level to Lead (in charge of SST's) and take on leadership role. Get promoted to staff position running their shifts
- Show significant progress working on their problems
- Work on GED
- Work on family relations

"PHASE II" (open-ended time limit):
- Clients begin process of looking for work
- Start going to college
- Start training programs
- Save money and pay off bills

"PHASE III"
- Prepare to graduate
- Set up "Aftercare Plan"
- Graduate and move to a positive environment/location or to a halfway house if needed.
- Come back for Aftercare sessions with their counselor

"MIRACLES"

I've mentioned Rod Bauer (Day House Program Director) was a former client, but we actually have several former clients with years of sobriety working at the Shelter and the "MIRACLES" Center. We have former clients working at seven other centers and halfway houses. They went to college, received degrees and wanted to get in the field to help give back.

One very special former client's name was Raul. I really liked Raul's spirit and determination. He was from Mexico and spoke English, but was embarrassed to speak. He had difficulty finding work because of the language barrier and also because of his older age. He stayed sober and helped many people for almost three years before relapsing back to drinking. He'd been drinking very heavy for about five weeks when we heard about it and went to see him. He was in horrible shape. I didn't recognize him at first, because he was so emaciated and was stuck in a dark corner of his apartment. He couldn't walk or talk. We took him back to the shelter. The guys showered him, the women got him clean clothes and I fed him. The next day we helped him sit up and he shared how proud he was to almost have three years of sobriety. He also shared he was so proud that we cared enough to come get him. I felt good too. But not long afterwards, Raul died suddenly. I, and everyone, was shaken by his death! What could we have done differently?

After praying about it for a couple of days and talking to his neighbors, we found out Raul's biggest fear was dying alone in his dark apartment. I realized that was what it was all about. We thought we were saving Raul's life, but what we were really doing was getting him out of that dirty, dark and lonely apartment so he could die with people who loved him. We were able to get him cleaned up and feeling good about himself, so he could leave this world in peace. "Raul touched many, many lives."

CHAPTER 24

THE PROBLEM

"THERE IS NO COMPETITION;
IT'S ALL GOD'S WORK.
WE JUST WANT TO SEE MORE
PEOPLE GET THE HELP
THEY NEED.

PRISONS ARE STOCKPILED WITH
ADDICTS/ALCOHOLICS.

I HAVE PERSONALLY KNOWN 37
PEOPLE WHO DIED
FROM SUICIDE."

We have 90 clients in the "MIRACLES" program today, which is good. The problem is, we have a very long waiting list to get into treatment. Over the years, I know at least a couple of men died while waiting to enter treatment or were sent to prison. Our waiting list at times is four to five months, which is very sad.

We need more treatment centers and they need to be developed along the lines of "MIRACLES." I've included the section about the components of our program so others may develop something similar. We are more than willing to help in any way we can, because this approach works and because there are so many men and women that need help!

We, the Siena/Francis House, "MIRACLES" Treatment Center, myself and all the counselors want to help, because the need is so very great. Any help we can give is totally free. There is no competition, it's all God's work, and we just want to see more people get the help they need.

In 28 years, I have personally known 37 people die from suicide. I have heard of countless others, but I have known 37 personally. Two of them were my cousins. I wish they could have gotten this gift of a new life. We as a society have to reach down and support more treatment centers and counselors to carry the message of hope and a new life.

One of my best friends, Art, (we sponsor each other) lives in Florida and he started up a couple of Halfway houses and was doing good with the alcoholics, but couldn't get any of the drug addicts to stay sober.

One very important, critical action plan that Art did was ask for help. Art recognized he didn't know how to work with addicts and found the humility and sincerity to ask how we were so successful. This is very important. He sought help from professionals who had the answers.

I hear all kinds of talk and ideas about how to treat methamphetamine, cocaine, narcotics and marijuana addicts. I personally know hundreds of methamphetamine addicts who are staying sober, but I've never had one of them ever tell me anyone starting up treatment centers asked them how they got sober. I am a recovering methamphetamine addict and I know how I got sober and that's what I modeled the "MIRACLES" Treatment Center after.

Today, I have an incredible staff that also have learned to stay sober and together we guide others into a new life. We don't try to reinvent the wheel; we just reach out, sharing what so many recovering addicts have discovered. Then we duplicate that process and add to it, not change it.

This message is so important, it's Life and Death. Art understood this and asked for help. I invited Art and three men who were running his houses to come spend a week with us to learn what we do. Today, Art and his friends have developed The Wilson House, a small treatment program for 12 men with one of the houses. They've graduated many addicts/alcoholics who have been able to get back with families, and several have moved into their halfway house to continue in their recovery process.

Art's success rate is very good, because he realized the men, especially addicts, needed a longer duration of treatment. He's developed the same family environment that we have. They, of course, have developed their own program, but they were able to build off of the success that Art observed at Siena/Francis.

The "Message" is if God is nudging you to develop a treatment program, to donate money or to help in any way, go for it.

Alcoholics and addicts are dying every day and the prisons are overflowing. If I can do the things I have accomplished, so can you. Especially if you remember that it wasn't me, it was God directing me. This is an extremely serious problem, and very few of you reading this book haven't been touched by addiction. Please take up the challenge and reach out to help. I have a poem I'd like to share with you:

"I SOUGHT
MY SOUL,
BUT MY SOUL
I COULD NOT SEE.

I SOUGHT
MY GOD,
BUT MY GOD
ELUDED ME.

I SOUGHT
MY BROTHER,
AND, IN HIM,
I FOUND
ALL THREE."

CHAPTER 25

TWO WORLDS

**Physical
World**

**Spiritual
World**

"THANK YOU GOD.
PLEASE GUIDE ME AND
SHOW ME THE WAY.
PLEASE OPEN MY EYES
AND MY HEART
TO RECEIVE YOUR GUIDANCE.
THANK YOU FOR ALL THE
WONDERFUL PEOPLE
YOU'VE PLACED INTO
MY LIFE TO TEACH ME
AND GUIDE ME.
THANK YOU
SO VERY, VERY MUCH
FOR ALLOWING ME
TO BE AN INSTRUMENT
FOR YOU
TO WORK THROUGH.
THY WILL BE DONE.
AMEN.

As far as I know, there is only one physical world, but I've learned life is being lived in two entirely different realms. Prior to getting sober and working on my spirituality, I thought some people were very religious or spiritual and some were not. I've always said I believe in God and I do, but I didn't live that way. God was the Creator, but He was "out there," aloof to us except maybe keeping score of all the bad things I've done.

Today I absolutely know that I can live worldly like I had all my life, or I can live spiritually. I'm amazed that we can be living side by side, seemingly doing the same things: going to work, raising families, etc., but operating from totally opposite worlds. I sincerely hope by writing this book, I raise the awareness of those of you who haven't realized this truth so you can begin living spiritually. It's truly exciting what God has planned for us. In the Bible, Jesus said,

> I shall send forth my angels and they shall gather my chosen ones from the farthest ends of the earth and heaven.... The world will be at ease – banquets, parties and weddings.
> Two men will be working together in the fields and one will be taken, the other left. Two women will be going about their household tasks; one will be taken the other left.
> So be prepared, for you don't know what day your Lord is coming.
> Just as a man can prevent trouble from thieves by keeping watch for them, so you can avoid trouble by always being ready for my unannounced return.
> Are you a wise and faithful servant of the Lord? Have I given you the task of managing my household, to feed my children day by day? Blessings on you if I return and find you
> faithfully doing your work. I will put such faithful ones in charge of everything I own. (Mt. 24: 31-47).

I don't believe God is vengeful. I believe He loves us enough to give us free will to choose to accept His grace. I'm so grateful I was able to be open for God to enter and replace my old self with this new self centered in Jesus.

Before sobriety, I believed that it was all up to me to accomplish anything. Whatever I wanted I could attain, if I worked hard enough. It was all up to me. Some people were just lucky and had been born rich or extremely capable and some of us weren't; bad break for us unlucky ones. I measured my worth by how my position, my possessions, my job, compared to others, when I was living "worldly."

I've found there is a completely different existence, that of living "spiritually." Not just believing in God, but realizing God has a plan for your life, my life. Not only does He have a plan, He has the whole thing mapped out. All God wants us to do is trust totally and completely in Him, trust that God will guide us, wants to guide us, and has been waiting for us to recognize His grace and flow.

Since I've become aware of this flow of God's will, I've been trying to go with it. This has been difficult, scary at times, painful at times, but the end result always gives me hope and a closer connection to Him.

I suppose it's easier for people who have lost everything, like alcoholics and addicts, because we've been beaten down into total desperation. Life seems hopeless, nothing's left. Faith and God are seemingly our last chance, and we reach for that seemingly flimsy lifeline. What looks like a weak thread turns out to be the strongest cable in the world pulling us up. It is God's hand.

The problem is retaining that knowledge and understanding. Alcoholics, addicts and others can lose everything: their families, jobs, homes, licenses, cars, friends, money, physical, mental and spiritual health and come to treatment absolutely bankrupt, in every way desperate, wanting help, willing to do whatever is necessary. Do you know what the first thing they get back is if they are not working hard on themselves? Ego!

If the Ego is allowed to come back, all of a sudden the addict is back in control. Ego is running the show and God is out the door. Once again, the addict takes credit for his/her success, and stops doing the simple basic things required for God's grace to enter and stay in our lives. Sometimes they can hold on and do well for various periods of time, but then they fall apart again. They've lost all once again and want help. It can be a vicious cycle, but if we work the 12 Steps we can keep grounded and stay in God's wonderful grace. So we have to be careful to not forget the past. I use my past experience to remind myself what happened to me when my ego ran the show.

**DEAR LORD,
TEACH
US
TO
LAUGH
AGAIN.
BUT PLEASE,
DON'T LET US
FORGET
WE CRIED!**

One of my biggest prayers is for God to wait to give me something until I am ready for it.

I had a wonderful wife, children, good jobs, a nice home, but I didn't appreciate and treasure those gifts. Instead, I misused and abused everything. As my life gets fuller and fuller, I want to make absolutely sure I appreciate everything and everybody. I truly ask God not to give me anything until I can appreciate and treasure whatever the gift is. Everything is a gift from God, anything good is from God. Whatever difficulties or bad things have happened in my life, God has used to help me grow closer to Him and rely more deeply on His grace. Everything that has happened in my life I've been able to use to be more than I was before, to grow as a man and as a human being.

Here is my prayer: "Thank you God, please guide me and show me the way. Please open my eyes and my heart to receive Your guidance. Thank You for all the wonderful people You've placed into my life to teach me and guide me. Thank You so very, very much for allowing me to be an instrument for You to work through. Thy will be done. Amen."

CHAPTER 26

ONE DAY AT A TIME

THANK GOD
FOR TODAY!

GOING WITH THE FLOW

Go with the flow. Let go of fear and your need to control. Relinquish anxiety. Let it slip away, as you dive into the river of the present moment, the river of your life, your place in the universe. Stop trying to force the direction. Try not to swim against the current, unless it is necessary for your survival. If you've been clinging to a branch at the riverside, let go. Let yourself move forward. Let yourself be moved forward. Avoid the rapids when possible. If you can't, stay relaxed. Staying relaxed can take you safely through fierce currents. If you go under for a moment, allow yourself to surface naturally. You will.

Don't think too hard about things. The flow is meant to be experienced. Within it, care for yourself. You are part of the flow, an important part. Work with the flow. Thrashing about isn't necessary. Let the flow help you care for yourself. Let it help you set boundaries, make decisions and get you where you need to be when it is time. You can trust the flow, and your part in it. Today, I will go with the flow.

-Melodie Beattie-
"Language of Letting Go"
July 8th

I wake up in the morning and make my bed. Making my bed is part of my recovery program. It's a very important part, because I can't miss seeing that I have a messed up bed and it's part of my recovery program to make it. This is a visible reminder of my program that: (1) I'm an alcoholic, (2) sobriety is a gift, but I need to work a recovery program, (3) I only have to stay sober for just today. I don't have to worry about the rest of my life, just today. I can handle that, especially with my support system and God.

After making the bed, I get on my knees and read, "The Upper Room" meditation for the day and read the suggested Bible reading. I write a letter to God, normally as a gratitude letter for all the things I'm grateful for today. I ask for God's guidance and get ready for work. I feed my horse, dog and cat. During the day, if I feel stressed or anxious I stop, say a prayer and talk to someone.

At least once a week I do a "mantra" form of meditation with the treatment group which is very energizing. I need to do it alone more often.

I usually attend four 12-Step meetings per week. I attend two A.A. meetings, chair a CODA (Co-Dependency) meeting and attend one CMA (Crystal Methamphetamine Anonymous) meeting.

Four days a week, I work out with my workout partners (I'm always training four or five guys). We push each other. We use the same basic principles with working out – supporting, motivating, and pushing each other. Working out is a great way of teaching how the program works in all areas of our lives. I've worked out lifting weights since I was 13 years old and I believe that knowledge helped me to stay sober. I knew that I couldn't work out real hard for a month and expect to look like Arnold over night. I knew that if I only worked out some of the time I wasn't going to get results. I knew that if I didn't put my whole heart and mind into and experience the pain I wasn't going to get results. I learned that when possible it's very beneficial to have work out partners. So I knew and understood the absolute importance of discipline, commitment, following directions and fellowship before I ever heard of A.A. or recovery.

When I drive in my block-long driveway, my big horse, Cutter, comes running up to the corral to meet me. I always give Cutter a big hug, morning and night. Cole, my black lab, and I go for a mile walk every night, regardless of the weather. Sometimes I'll let him come in and watch some television with me. My cat, Kisses, is always there and likes to follow me around my acreage. Having animals is very relaxing and nurturing. They teach me a lot about unconditional love, being responsible and caring about others.

I always say my prayers before eating. I've learned that at the homeless shelter. I learned it at home, but I've gained a greater understanding from watching our guests. Sometimes throughout the day I might get busy and forget to pray, so mealtimes are a perfect reminder to slow down and pray.

What I'm not doing well at is getting to sleep on time; I have a tendency to stay up too late but I'm working on that.

At night I say my prayers and usually do some self-hypnosis, meditation or Gratitudes, thanking God for another sober, wonderful day.

My daughter, Billie, son-in-law Keith, and my grandsons live with me and that is a real gift. Billie and I never had the opportunity to live together when she was growing up, so it's been wonderful. She started college with my encouragement and a few times I had to drop her off at school or pick her up and we both appreciated the significance.

My grandchildren and kids have a place they can visit and enjoy themselves. I can't change the past, but we can sure enjoy the present time and the future.

"One day at a time" has turned into over 28 years of living and doing the best I can for that day.

Truly, Life has never been so good!

PART TWO

THE PROCESS

> ## "FAITH WITHOUT WORKS IS DEAD."

In Part One of this book, I shared my journey and trust it helped and inspired you to have hope. I also pray it inspired you to take some action.

Now I want to share some of the process I've learned and the actions I've taken personally to get into and continue my own recovery.

The Bible says, "Faith without works is dead." The Big Book explains that verse means faith alone will not get us anywhere. We have to be willing to take <u>ACTION</u>.

Part Two of this book is, as Paul Harvey says, "The rest of the story."

CHAPTER 27

WE NEED MORE TREATMENT CENTERS

BULLETIN:

"OUR PRISONS ARE OVERFLOWING WITH UNTREATED ALCOHOLICS/ADDICTS."

"For unto whomever much is given, of him much shall be required." (Luke 12:48).

Eppley Treatment Centers had five treatment centers and 46 counselors in our heyday. We were able to help thousands of patients and their families. Eppley hasn't been in existence for 15 years now, because managed care and insurance companies wouldn't pay for chemical dependence treatment, especially inpatient. Hardly a day goes by, if any, that I don't run into several former patients who went through Eppley and are living wonderful lives.

Hopefully the big experiment of not paying for inpatient treatment is about over and we'll again see treatment centers opening up. The prisons are overflowing with untreated alcoholics and addicts.

It is my sincere prayer that this book will help wake up our wonderful country, the United States, to see that we have failed in this area.

"WE DON'T NEED MORE AND LARGER PRISONS. WE NEED TO BRING BACK THE SUCCESSFUL TREATMENT CENTERS AND REALIZE WE'VE BEEN STOCKPILING OUR SICK IN PRISONS."

Come on America! We can do this! We have to do this!

DENIAL is the biggest problem of the alcoholic and addict; it's the biggest problem for the families. Families can't recognize the problem unless they get help and get some education to understand the symptoms. Guess what? It's even bigger than that. Our whole society has not recognized it.

Seriously, how many families have not been affected by drugs and alcohol or other addiction, such as gambling, sex and food? I believe a large percentage of our population has been personally affected, and certainly all of us have from a society perspective.

There are a lot of misperceptions out there that treatment doesn't work, but it's the minority saying that. Yes, there are treatment centers that don't do a good job, but I know good inpatient 12-Step centers do work! I'm talking about treatment centers and H.W.H. (halfway houses), but it should be noted that many people don't need treatment because they've been able to get sober through 12-step meetings, reading the Big Book, getting a sponsor and working the steps. I did need the help of treatment, as many of us do, but not all of us. I am glad I went to treatment because it gave me time to look deeper into myself.

12-Step Programs Work:

Alcoholics Anonymous, Narcotics Anonymous, Cocaine Anonymous, Crystal Meth Anonymous, CoDependence Anonymous and AL ANON. The startling actual facts about the growth of 12-Step programs are phenomenal. A.A. started in 1935 in Akron, Ohio and since that time has increased to a worldwide membership of two million or more, with nearly 100,800 groups meeting in approximately 150 countries around the world (Big Book, Foreword to 4th Edition). Whenever I travel anywhere, I always make it a point to attend A.A. meetings. Besides the United States, I've attended A.A. in Mexico, Belize, Padre Island and the Bahamas. There's usually a poster up that says, "There are no strangers here, just friends you haven't met yet." Thank God.

In Omaha, Nebraska, in 1979 there were 46 A.A. meetings. In 2006, there are 560 A.A. meetings in the Omaha area. This doesn't count all the other 12-Step meetings that have started up. That increase is 12 times the original amount of meetings in 27 years. There is no shortage of alcoholics or addicts, so at that same rate of expansion, we'll have 12x560=6720 meetings a week in the Omaha area within another 27 years. That represents an incredibly successful rate of recovery.

The prisons are going to keep growing at a tremendous rate if we don't get more treatment centers. Everyone knows that it is extremely costly to house and board prisoners. Let's spend that money getting them good help – we need more treatment centers!

CHAPTER 28

BASICS OF A GOOD TREATMENT CENTER

"EACH OF THESE CLIENTS HAS
AFFECTED THEIR FAMILIES AND
LOVED ONES
AND HAS MADE
THEIR LIVES
SO MUCH BETTER."

"GOD, PLEASE MAKE US
TO BE
GOOD INSTRUMENTS
FOR YOU
TO WORK THROUGH."

To begin with, I am definitely a "12-Steps" centered man due to the 100% success rate of my own recovery. I continue on a daily basis to be in awe of the "Gift" of my own recovery and so is everyone who knew me in the past.

I also use the "12 Traditions" of A.A. as best I can in the management and operations of the treatment centers I've been involved in developing. The 12 Steps have already been shown, and I'll go into more detail in the next chapter, but I will also list the 12 Traditions:

1. Our common welfare should come first; personal recovery depends upon A.A. unity.
2. For our group purpose there is but one ultimate authority – a loving God as He may express Himself in our group conscience. Our leaders are but trusted servants; they do not govern.
3. The only requirement for A.A. membership is a desire to stop drinking.
4. Each group should be autonomous except in matters affecting other groups or A.A. as a whole.
5. Each group has but one primary purpose – to carry its message to the alcoholic who still suffers.
6. An A.A. group ought never endorse, finance or lend the A.A. name to any related facility or outside enterprise, lest problems of money, property and prestige divert us from our primary purpose.
7. Every A.A. group ought to be fully self-supporting, declining outside contributions.
8. Alcoholics Anonymous should remain forever nonprofessional, but our service centers may employ special workers.
9. A.A., as such, ought never be organized; but we may create service boards or committees directly responsible to those they serve.
10. Alcoholics Anonymous has no opinion on outside issues; hence the A.A. name ought never be drawn into public controversy.

11. Our public relations policy is based on attraction rather than promotion; we need always maintain personal anonymity at the level of press, radio and films.
12. Anonymity is the spiritual foundation of all our Traditions, ever reminding us to place principles before personalities.

(Twelve Steps and Twelve Traditions)

These traditions are incredible and, I believe, also divinely inspired. Any business can benefit from using those that fit. Our treatment center tries to employ them and the principles embodied in them.

There is much research that says treatment centers don't work or have little success. The reason for this is because many treatment centers are not effective. Many so called treatment centers are not even 12-Step based.

Many 12 Step C.D. treatment programs look the same on paper when they describe what they do. Some of these centers have very poor results, while others, and especially the "MIRACLES" Treatment Recovery Center that I am the Director of, have incredible rates. What are the reasons for the discrepancies and what components need to be addressed?

- Actually working all 12 Steps
- Developing discipline
- Being firm
- Support
- Role models
- Length of treatment time
- Community 12-Step involvement
- Therapists who are working their own recovery programs
- Medical help
- Developing spirituality
- Psychiatric counseling and medications if needed
- Grief therapy
- Employment training
- Building self esteem and confidence
- Learning to reach out and help others
- Developing coping skills

- Identifying negative/erroneous belief systems
- Love and understanding
- Hope
- Learning to be honest
- Help to recognize insane thinking
- Understanding relapse prevention warning signs
- Developing a solid foundation of reading the Big Book, 12x12, meditation books
- Calling sponsor regularly
- Attending 12-Step meetings (I like a minimum of three per week, quite often daily at first)
- Prayer.

Over the years, I've had the privilege of being part of starting several treatment centers. I'm happy and proud to say they all have been very successful. I've been blessed to see hundreds, actually thousands, of our clients get into recovery and experience the joys that life has to offer. What is even more wonderful is that each of these clients/patients has affected their families and loved ones and made their family's lives so much better. I'm talking really about thousands of people who have somehow been affected by my work and my recovery.

Don't think I'm getting egotistical, because I'm not....it's not me. It truly is not me. I couldn't do that. It's God and how He can use us to be His instruments. My biggest prayer always is for God to use me and my co-workers to be good instruments for Him to work through. I can testify to His wondrous power and miracles. I know what I can do by myself. That's all the pain and misery I caused before I was given the gift of recovery. One of my favorite thoughts is, "To whom much has been given, much is expected." I've been given so much!

A branch of a national organization in Nebraska that educates people on 12-Step programs is called Nebraska Recovery Network, which is dedicated to getting the message out that recovery is happening everywhere. The 12-Step programs are anonymous for very important spiritual reasons, but because of this anonymity, society really doesn't realize how many millions of people are enjoying sobriety and being very productive members of society.

Instead, what we hear is a lot of disgruntled people who tried half-heartedly to get sober and then blamed their failure on A.A. and other 12-Step programs. The Big Book is very clear that half-measures will get us nowhere and especially not sober. So this organization's sole purpose is to carry the 12-Step message of A.A. to as many people as possible, letting them know that the 12-Step program, when followed wholeheartedly, changes lives. If you would like more information about this organization, the telephone number and e-mail address are listed in the Reference section of this book.

Part of the motivation for this book is to heighten 12-Step awareness and also to alert people that we need to re-develop good, affordable 12-Step treatment centers.

CHAPTER 29

12 STEPS AND PRINCIPLES

> "I DO BELIEVE
> THE ROAD
> GETS NARROWER,
> BUT
> THERE'S A SECRET.
> AT THE TOP
> GOD HAS AN ESCALATOR,
> WHEN
> WE ARE IN
> HIS FLOW
> DOING HIS WILL"

I'm not going to get deep into the 12 Steps of A.A. I'll just go through them briefly as they are shared in the A.A. Big Book and the 12x12. I will share that they are so powerful; I truly believe they were divinely inspired. It's important to explain the steps are written in the past tense because they are being shared to explain what the founding fathers of A.A. did to achieve sobriety.

Step 1: **"We admitted we were powerless over alcohol – that our lives had become unmanageable."**

Step 1 basically says that I can't stop using or whatever the particular problem is that I can't stop doing. I want to stop, but I do it anyway, even though it's causing serious problems in my life. Even St. Paul struggled with this problem. In Romans 7:15 he says, "I do not understand what I do. For what I want to do I do not do, but what I hate I do."

Step 2: **"Came to believe that a power greater than ourselves could restore us to sanity."**

Paraphrased, it means I know I can't, but I totally believe God can through this program. I've always believed in God, but I didn't understand that He truly is right there and wants to help us. I wrote out a list of all the people I knew in recovery that had serious problems but eventually their lives or problems worked out for the best. It was a long list and helped me believe that regardless of what it looks like, things will be okay. Maybe not how I think they should be, but God truly will guide me through whatever and I'll be okay.

Step 3: **"Made a decision to turn our will and our lives over to the care of God, as we understood Him."**

The question is, am I going to truly turn my life (everything, as it is at this moment) over to God and my will, my wants, my control, my running the show? Am I going to let go and follow His directions? Many people get stuck here because they don't take action. I like a ridiculous story about three frogs sitting on a lily pad in the middle of a pond. One of the frogs decided to jump off. The question is, how many frogs are left sitting on the lily pad. Two? Three? None? The answer is three, because in order to get off the lily pad, the frog would have to take the action of jumping off. So the first part of Step 3 is making a decision, but the second part is taking actions, such as working the steps, going to meetings, reading the Big Book, calling a sponsor and helping others.

Step 4: **"Made a searching and fearless moral inventory of ourselves."**

No secrets, write it all down. This is an extremely important step if we are to truly change. I don't believe God is going to change anything until we are fully aware of our shortcomings, otherwise we'll just take full credit and not see the need for God in our lives. So we write it all down, both the negatives and the positives. There are many good formats to use that can help you do this. In the Index, I've included the one the counselors and chaplains at the old Eppley Chemical Dependence Treatment Center developed.

Step 5: **"Admitted to God, to ourselves and to another human being the exact nature of our wrongs."**

I'm a Catholic and we go to confession to ask for God's forgiveness. Step 5 is not a confession; we believe God has already forgiven us and this step is designed to help us forgive ourselves, to understand that we've been very sick, out of control, lost and confused. Secrets will keep us sick, but talking and sharing will begin the process to set us free. In many of my college psychology and counseling classes we discussed how strong a hold on us our pasts have and that made sense. It wasn't until a few years later when I got sober and did a thorough 4th and 5th Step that I realized the significance. After completing my first 4th and 5th Step, I found my thinking totally changing. I wasn't so angry. I became more understanding, more trusting, more forgiving. I was amazed by the changes taking place in me.

Steps 6: **"Were entirely ready to have God remove all these defects of character."**

My sponsor told me he thought most people got drunk over this step. I was confused because it didn't seem like much, so I studied it. I found Steps 6 and 7 to be very spiritual. Step 6 basically says that any real changes are going to come from God. Our part is to become aware and try to make ourselves ready.

What happens is, if we think it's all up to us, we get discouraged if we keep having the same problem over and over. If addicted people allow ourselves to get totally discouraged, we could give up and go back to using.

What we need to do is follow through working the 12 Steps, pray, and trust that God is in charge. When I celebrated my five-year sobriety birthday, I became upset and angry because I realized if I didn't go to meetings, work the Steps, pray and help others, I'd be right back where I was before I got here. Subconsciously, I believed that by the time I got five years of sobriety I'd be well. I'd still go to meetings, not because I had to, but to be there for others.

What I realized eventually is that it's okay, in fact it's wonderful, that God made us to need each other. The powerlessness in Step 1, the gift of being restored in Step 2 and the decision and action of Step 3 will always be required throughout my life. Those three steps keep me centered and aware of my need for God and others. So really now I realize that my character defects in some ways are gifts that bring me closer to God. Steps 6 and 7 are really refined Steps 1, 2 and 3 working on ourselves.

Personally, I make myself ready by developing a very strong support system that will help keep me on the right path and point out any problems they are aware of. They also can trust that I'll do the same for them. We can have the best intentions, but find ourselves out in left field if we don't check our thinking and motives out with our support system.

Step 7: Humbly asked Him to remove our shortcomings.

These two wonderful Steps 6 and 7 are sometimes called the "visible steps" because during this part of the process people can actually see the changes taking place, often before we ourselves can see them. Basically to me this step is an acknowledgement or honoring of God as our Creator and the Source of my power.

One of my favorite prayers is the 7th Step Prayer (p. 76 of the Big Book):

> "MY CREATOR, I AM NOW WILLING
> THAT YOU SHOULD HAVE ALL OF ME,
> GOOD AND BAD.
> I PRAY THAT YOU
> NOW REMOVE FROM ME
> EVERY SINGLE DEFECT OF CHARACTER
> WHICH STANDS IN THE WAY
> OF MY USEFULNESS TO YOU
> AND MY FELLOWS.
> GRANT ME STRENGTH,
> AS I GO OUT FROM HERE,
> TO DO YOUR BIDDING. AMEN."

I remember a movie with John Candy jumping in bed with his girlfriend. He suddenly jumped back out of bed, took his hat and covered up a statue of the Virgin Mary. I couldn't help but laugh because that's so human and how I used to be. If I was doing something I should not have been doing, I would kind of hide out from God until I was being good.

I had it all backwards and this prayer helped me to understand. I need to go to God as I am, good and bad, and let God do the changing His way.

Step 8: Made a list of all persons we had harmed, and became willing to make amends to them all.

We write it all down! Up to now, we've been working on ourselves but now we are going to begin working on our relationships. Finally we're ready to begin becoming much more productive members of society. Some of our wrongs may not be amenable, but we write it all down.

Step 9: Made direct amends to such people whenever possible, except when to do so would injure them or others.

Steps 8 and 9 are the amends steps. These steps are concerned with trying to make amends for the wreckage of our past, willful, self-centered lives. We made a list of all the people we have harmed and with whom we need to make amends. But we check our list out with our sponsors, making sure that our disclosures won't cause someone more pain.

On page 83 of the Big Book it says:

> Yes, there is a long period of reconstruction ahead. We must take the lead. A remorseful mumbling that we are sorry won't fill the bill at all. We ought to sit down with the family and frankly analyze the past as we now see it, being very careful not to criticize them. Their defects may be glaring, but the chances are that our own actions are partly responsible. So we clean house with the family, asking each morning in meditation that our Creator show us the way to patience, tolerance, kindliness and love.
>
> The spiritual life is not a theory. We have to live it. Unless one's family expresses a desire to live upon spiritual principles we think we ought not to urge them. We should not talk incessantly to them about spiritual matters. They will change in time. Our behavior will convince them more than our words. We must remember that ten or twenty years of drunkenness would make a skeptic out of anyone.
>
> There may be some wrongs we can never fully right. We don't worry about them if we can honestly say to ourselves that we would right them if we could. Some people cannot be seen – we send them an honest letter. And there may be a valid reason for postponement in some cases. But we don't delay if it can be avoided. We should be sensible, tactful, considerate and humble without being servile or scraping. As God's people we stand on our feet; we don't crawl before anyone.

What will happen if we work these steps? "The Promises" (p. 83-84 of the Big Book) states:

THE PROMISES

"If we are painstaking about this phase of our development, we will be amazed before we are halfway through. We are going to know a new freedom and a new happiness. We will not regret the past nor wish to shut the door on it. We will comprehend the word serenity and we will know peace. No matter how far down the scale we have gone, we will see how our experience can benefit others. That feeling of uselessness and self-pity will disappear. We will lose interest in selfish things and gain interest in our fellows. Self-seeking will slip away. Our whole attitude and outlook upon life will change. Fear of people and of economic insecurity will leave us. We will intuitively know how to handle situations which used to baffle us. We will suddenly realize that God is doing for us what we could not do for ourselves.

Are these extravagant promises? We think not. They are being fulfilled among us – sometimes quickly, sometimes slowly. They will always materialize if we work for them."

The fact that I am writing this book attests to the fact that the promises indeed do come true. The part of the promises I really hung onto was "….sometimes quickly, sometimes slowly." I was very sick and the process for me to change seemed very slow, but it wasn't. I just had no comprehension of how sick, mentally and spiritually, I was when I first got into treatment. Now however, I truly have a life and am a very productive member of the human race. Today I have a calling, as do we all, to reach out and help others experience the gift of this world God has blessed us with and to help make this a better world.

Step 10: "**Continued to take personal inventory and when we were wrong, promptly admitted it.**"

Thank God for this step, because it tells me I am not perfect. At times I may make mistakes or act inappropriately, but when I realize it I can stop and make amends. Sometimes this can be painful due to false pride and ego, but with humility we can make amends and take whatever corrective measures are necessary.

> # "HUMILITY = TEACHABILITY BE TEACHABLE. REMAIN TEACHABLE."

On page 86 of the Big Book is a very simple and good daily inventory to take anytime throughout the day and at night time. I have learned to keep things simple and this inventory does that.

> When we retire at night, we constructively review our day. Were we resentful, selfish, dishonest or afraid? Do we owe an apology? Have we kept something to ourselves which should be discussed with another person at once? Were we kind and loving toward all? What could we have done better? Were we thinking of what we could do for others, of what we could pack into the stream of life? But we must be careful not to drift into worry, remorse or morbid reflection, for that would diminish our usefulness to others. After making our review we ask God's forgiveness and inquire what corrective measures should be taken.

On awakening let us think about the twenty-four hours ahead. We consider our plans for the day. Before we begin, we ask God to direct our thinking, especially asking that it be divorced from self-pity, dishonest or self-seeking motives. Under these conditions, we can employ our mental faculties with assurance, for after all God gave us brains to use. Our thought-life will be placed on a much higher plane when our thinking is cleared of wrong motives.

In thinking about our day we may face indecision. We may not be able to determine which course to take. Here we ask God for inspiration, an intuitive thought or a decision. We relax and take it easy. We don't struggle. We are often surprised how the right answers come after we have tried this for awhile.

Today I try to live my life as if I live in a glass house. If I catch myself doing anything I feel I need to be secretive or ashamed to tell others about, that's my clue to stop. Honesty and living in the light is the only right policy.

How I act at home, at work and at play is all the same. I try to watch my language and work the principles wherever I am. So what you see or what you read here is exactly what you get. I actually love myself because I've been working hard to be the best me I can be. I'm so fortunate to have many, many friends that have helped me on this journey.

<u>Step 11</u>: Sought through prayer and meditation to improve our conscious contact with God as we understood Him, praying only for knowledge of His will for us and the power to carry that out.

Step 11 is concerned with continuing to work on our spirituality through prayer and meditation. Remembering to pray for knowledge of His will and the power (grace) to follow through. On page 99 of the 12x12 is a wonderful prayer in A.A. that is known as the St. Francis of Assisi Prayer:

ST. FRANCIS OF ASSISI PRAYER

"Lord, make me an instrument of your peace.
Where there is hatred . . . let me sow love.
Where there is injury . . . pardon.
Where there is doubt . . . faith.
Where there is despair . . .hope.
Where there is darkness . . . light.
Where there is sadness . . .joy.
Divine Master,
grant that I may not so much seek
To be consoled . . .as to console.
To be understood . . .as to understand.
To be loved . . . as to love.
For it is in giving . . .that we receive.
It is in pardoning, that we are pardoned.
It is in dying . . .that we are born to
eternal life."

What we seek in this Step is a greater awareness of God, His power and His peace that tells us everything is okay. Just trust in God. This is a wonderful prayer, and I like to contemplate its meaning. The concepts are goals to work towards, gifts to offer to others, to our loved ones, to everyone.

The idea is to try to understand rather than to be understood. When I find myself in a disagreement with someone and at a stalemate, I remember, "Seek to understand rather than to be understood."

Step 12: **Having had a spiritual awakening as a result of these steps, we tried to carry this message to alcoholics/addicts, and to practice these principles in all our affairs.**

This step contains the greatest promise of all the promises. "Having had a spiritual awakening as the result of these steps, we tried to carry this message to alcoholics/addicts, and to practice these principles in all our affairs."

What an incredibly bold promise that we will have a spiritual awakening if we sincerely work these steps. I can promise you it's true. I know, because I've seen it happen to everyone who has been willing to work this 12-Step program.

We are asked the same thing that Jesus asked the apostles: to go out and carry the message of new life, to be born again.

In the Twelve Steps and Twelve Traditions (12x12) book on pages 106 and 107, this awakening and message is described:

> When a man or woman has a spiritual awakening, the most important meaning of it is that he has now become able to do, feel, and believe that which he could not do before on his unaided strength and resources alone. He has been granted a gift which amounts to a new state of consciousness and being. He has been set on a path which tells him he is really going somewhere, that life is not a dead end, not something to be endured or mastered. In a very real sense, he has been transformed, because he has laid hold of a source of strength, which, in one way or another, he had hitherto denied himself. He finds himself in possession of a degree of honesty, tolerance, unselfishness, peace of mind, and love of which he had thought himself quite incapable. What he has received is a free gift, and yet usually, at least in some small part, he has made himself ready to receive it.
>
> A.A.'s manner of making ready to receive this gift lies in the practice of the Twelve Steps. "When we sincerely practice these steps, all sorts of remarkable things followed. We had a new employer. Being all powerful, He provided what we needed if we kept close to Him and performed His work well. Established on such a footing, we became less and less interested in ourselves, our little plans and our designs.

More and more we became interested in seeing what we could contribute to life. As we felt new power flow in, as we enjoyed peace of mind, as we discovered we could face life successfully, as we became conscious of His presence, we began to lose our fear of today, tomorrow or the hereafter. We were reborn (Big Book, page 63).

Principles of the Program:

"Practice these principles in all our affairs" is the intent of Step 12. We are charged to go out into society and help make this a better world and we can and are doing that. Today there are several million people throughout the world living these principles. We have to live them if we are to stay sober and enjoy life. These are the special attributes that working each Step develops in our lives:

PRINCIPLES OF RECOVERY

Step 1: **Honesty**: Everything starts with honesty at the core of our lives

Step 2: **Hope**: This is the cornerstone of life.

Step 3: **Faith**: Faith is the glue that holds it all together.

Step 4: **Courage**: Real courage to stand for what we believe – to cry, laugh, feel, live.

Step 5: **Integrity**: A person of integrity is someone who can be trusted and relied on to be true.

Step 6: **Willingness**: The key to change, to be open to new possibilities.

Step 7: **Humility**: Being teachable, knowing that God is truly in charge and all that we are and have is a gift from Him.

Step 8: **Brotherly Love**: We are all God's children, brothers and sisters, so love one another.

Step 9: **Justice**: Doing what is right and being fair.

Step 10: **Perseverance**: Don't give up. Be persistent. Live in God's strength.

Step 11:   **Spiritual Awareness**: The knowledge that God is in control, loves us and is always with us

Step 12: **Service**: Jesus said the two greatest commandments are, "Love the Lord your God with all your heart, soul and mind. This is the first and greatest commandment. The second most important is similar: Love your neighbor as much as you love yourself. All the other commandments and all the demands of the prophets stem from these two laws. Keep only these and you will find you are obeying all the others" (Matthew 22: 37-40).

Of course these principles are all from the Bible and many people are able to learn these through their churches. I wasn't able to hear, or learn or apply these ideas until I first was beaten down enough to listen.

Many people, most alcoholics and addicts didn't realize what we were doing prior to getting into recovery. We thought we were out there trying to succeed, to get jobs, promotions, start families or complete school. That wasn't what we were doing at all.

What we were doing was getting beaten down bad enough, experiencing all the pain and despair necessary to be able to enter the toughest God program there is. And we did a good job. We could not have gotten to this point in our lives if we hadn't gone through every single experience it took to get rid of self-will so we could be open to God's will and allow His grace to enter our lives. As I've said, I'm sad for all the pain I've caused others and myself, but it took every single bit of it to get me to this point. I couldn't have gotten here any other way.

Thank God we are finally here. Now let's see what wonders God has in store for us. We've been trying to swim upstream, when God has a perfect flow going downstream.

I do believe the road gets narrower the higher we aspire, but there's a secret. At the top, God has an escalator when we are in His flow. These steps were first developed for alcoholics, but we don't have to be alcoholic or have any addictions to work these steps. These steps are the best blueprint for living life and working on problems that I have ever discovered. Let's all start today to live these steps and practice these principles in all our affairs, especially at home with our loved ones.

CHAPTER 30

ANGER AND RESENTMENT

"IT IS AS IF THERE ARE
TWO WOLVES INSIDE ME
ONE IS GOOD,
ONE IS FULL OF ANGER.
SOMETIMES IT IS HARD
TO LIVE WITH
TWO WOLVES INSIDE ME.
THE BOY LOOKED INTENTLY INTO
HIS
GRANDFATHER'S EYES
AND ASKED,
'WHICH ONE WINS?'
THE GRANDFATHER SMILED AND
SAID,
'THE ONE I FEED.'"

Nothing is more dangerous for an alcoholic or addict than resentment. **"It is our number one offender. It destroys us more than anything else. From it stems all forms of spiritual disease for we have been not only mentally and physically ill, we have been spiritually sick"** (pg 64 in Big Book).

This is true for anyone. A life which includes deep resentment leads only to futility and unhappiness. When we allow ourselves to get caught up in anger and resentment, we shut ourselves off from the sunlight of the Spirit.

So we can't afford to get lost in resentment. Over the years, I've had to deal with a lot of anger and resentment at times; Thank God I realized it was a luxury I couldn't afford. When I first got sober, I had two big resentments that I had to work through or fall back to my disease. The first one was toward my ex-father-in-law and the second toward a brother.

With my father-in-law, Jim, I had refused to go over to their house toward the end of my marriage. My reasons: he was a big loud mouth, didn't have to work and didn't give my ex-wife her inheritance. In the Big Book chapter "Freedom from Bondage," p. 552, it says:

> If you have a resentment you want to be free of, if you will pray for that person or the thing that you resent, you will be free. If you will ask in prayer for everything you want for yourself to be given to them, you will be free. Ask for their health, their prosperity, their happiness, and you will be free. Even when you don't really want it for them, and your prayers are only words and you don't mean it, go ahead and do it anyway. Do it every day for two weeks and you will find you have come to mean it and do want it for them, and you will realize that where you used to feel bitterness and resentment and hatred, you now feel compassionate understanding and love.

I was desperate and willing, so I tried it. I prayed for my father-in-law every day and after five or six days I remembered I owed him about $3,000 I had borrowed. That was what it was all about. I had manufactured all those lies I believed to cover up my guilt. Once I figured this out, I called him and set up a payment plan.

My father-in-law was a wonderful man. I miss him a lot, since his death many years ago. He became one of my strongest support persons, always writing me cards of encouragement. I did pay him back financially, but I could never pay him back for his support. In his will, he gave me my oldest son's college football championship ring.

The resentment toward my brother was much different. I prayed for him every day for over a year. I prayed to forgive him for all the wrongs he committed against me. One day I woke up and understood I didn't need to forgive him. That wasn't what it was all about. All of a sudden I realized that we had both been insane from our alcoholism and drug addiction. We had both done things that hurt each other. It must have been tough to have a big brother who was as crazy as I was and always just a little step ahead. He was the toughest person I knew next to me and we had some very severe fights. My brother is in recovery today. He went through some of the same process and feelings that I experienced and today we've made amends. We love each other and, if needed, we will be there for each other. All of us brothers feel that way.

Over the years, I had problems with some co-workers and bosses.

> # "WHEN THE PUPIL IS READY, THE TEACHER ARRIVES"
> (old Chinese proverb).

I didn't feel like I was ready or needed any lessons, but the teachers arrived, causing me to work really hard on myself. Each person helped me work on my shortcomings, which in turn prepared me for the next difficult person, and eventually to live life with serenity and peace. Without each lesson, I wouldn't have been able to handle the next more difficult situation. Another paragraph from he Big Book, pages 66 and 67 says:

> This was our course: we realized that the people who wronged us were perhaps spiritually sick. Though we did not like their symptoms and the way these disturbed us, they, like ourselves, were sick too. We asked God to help us show them the same tolerance, pity and patience that we would cheerfully grant a sick friend. When a person offended, we said to ourselves, 'This is a sick person. How can I be helpful to him/her? God save me from being angry. Thy will be done.
>
> We avoid retaliation or argument. We wouldn't treat sick people that way. If we do, we destroy our chance of being helpful. We cannot be helpful to all people, but at least God will show us how to take a kindly and tolerant view to each and every one.

Those two readings have been extremely helpful for me. A couple of times I actually needed to write out those paragraphs using the offending person's name. I was so angry that I couldn't stand thinking about them, but I could read about them. The first couple of days I pulled that paper out and read it about 100 times. I laugh about it now, but it worked then. The main thing I try to remember is ultimately resentment and anger all comes back to me. How important is it compared to my serenity or happiness? I talk about it, pray about it and trust in God and get back into what's in front of me to do.

The Serenity Prayer also helps. I made this Serenity Prayer plaque in treatment in 1978.

Once a girlfriend tricked me out of $800 when we broke up and I was upset and angry. I complained to my sponsor, Joe, and he asked me how much my serenity was worth. I didn't like that question, but he wanted to know if it was worth $800. I reluctantly agreed it was worth much more than $800. It was more valuable than anything! BUT!! No buts. Joe provided me with a new insight to look at the situation. I thought that money was mine, it was in my bank account, but evidently God just had me saving that money for her; it really wasn't mine. I was surprised and a little sad, because I thought it was mine.

Another time, I was having difficulty with a co-worker who at times was very angry and stressed. She didn't understand boundaries, and at times was rude and very controlling. I was letting her behaviors really upset me, so I went to see my therapist. She had problems, but I was making her problems mine and then responding in anger. During an EMDR (Eye Movement Desensitization and Reprocessing) session, I was able to change my perceptions and reactions. I come from a family of three generations who worked for the Union Pacific railroad and I visualized being on a train looking out the window at some unpleasant scenery going by. I just watched it and waved goodbye.

It was a good coping strategy for my co-workers also when that person was into her negative behaviors. We just waved goodbye in our minds and didn't stop to get off the train. It just didn't have anything to do with us, so we didn't buy into it.

A story I read years ago talked about a passenger in an airplane. If she looked out the window on the right side of the plane, she saw an enormous storm cloud, black and full of lightning. If she looked out the window on the left side of the plane, she saw blue sky and brilliant sunshine. She chose which window to look out of.

Another way of looking at our thoughts is expressed in an old Native American story shared here:

A NATIVE AMERICAN LESSON

An old Grandfather said to his grandson, who came to him with anger at a schoolmate who had done him an injustice, "Let me tell you a story. I too, at times, have felt a great hate for those who have taken so much, with no sorrow for what they do. But hate wears you down, and does not hurt your enemy. It is like taking poison and wishing your enemy would die. I have struggled with these feelings many times."

He continued, "It is as if there are two wolves inside me; one is good and does no harm. He lives in harmony with all around him and does not take offense when no offense was intended. He will only fight when it is right to do so, and in the right way. But the other wolf, ah! He is full of anger! The littlest thing will set him into a fit of temper. He fights everyone, all the time, for no reason. He cannot think because his anger and hate are so great. It is helpless anger, for his anger will change nothing.

Sometimes it is hard to live with these two wolves inside me, for both of them try to dominate my spirit." The boy looked intently into his Grandfather's eyes and asked, "Which one wins, Grandfather?" The Grandfather smiled and said, "The one I feed."

In the Big Book on pages 450-452, it's said in a different way, but is the same idea:

> Instead of seeing what was good about my wife, I began to focus on her defects. The more I focused my mind on her defects, the more they grew and multiplied. Every defect I pointed out to her became greater and greater. Each time I told her she was a nothing, she receded a little more into nowhere. The more I drank, the more she wilted.
> A.A. has given me a new pair of glasses. I can again focus on my wife's good qualities and watch them grow and grow.
> I can do the same thing with an A.A. meeting. The more I focus my mind on its defects –late start, long drunkalogues, and cigarette smoke – the worse the meeting becomes. But when I try to see what I can add to the meeting, rather than what I can get out of it, and when I focus my mind on what's good about it, rather than what's wrong with it, the meeting keeps getting better and better. When I focus on what's good today, I have a good day, and when I focus on what's bad, I have a bad day. If I focus on a problem, the problem increases; if I focus on the answer, the answer increases.
> Perhaps the best thing of all for me is to remember that my serenity is inversely proportional to my expectations. The higher my expectations of other people are, the lower is my serenity. I can watch my serenity level rise when I discard my expectations. But then my "rights" try to move in,
> and they, too, can force my serenity level down. I have to discard my "rights," as well as my expectations, by asking myself, "How important is it, really? How important is it compared to my serenity, my emotional sobriety?" And when I place more value on my serenity and sobriety than on anything else, I can maintain them at a higher level – at least for the time being.

CHAPTER 31

GRIEF

> ## "GOD SAID,
> ## 'BILL, BE STILL.
> ## I DON'T LIKE YOU BEING
> ## ANGRY AT ME,
> ## AND I KNOW
> ## YOU ARE HURTING.'"

BROKEN DREAMS

"AS CHILDREN BRING THEIR BROKEN TOYS
WITH TEARS FOR US TO MEND, I BROUGHT
MY BROKEN DREAMS TO GOD BECAUSE HE
WAS MY FRIEND.

BUT THEN INSTEAD OF LEAVING HIM IN PEACE
TO WORK ALONE, I HUNG AROUND AND TRIED
TO HELP WITH WAYS THAT WERE MY OWN.

AT LAST I SNATCHED THEM BACK AND CRIED,
'HOW CAN YOU BE SO SLOW?' 'MY CHILD,' HE
SAID, '
WHAT COULD I DO?
YOU NEVER LET THEM GO.'"

Grief is such an important aspect of people's lives by the time they get to treatment that I'm going to share a paper I've written about grief and healing.

Childhood trauma, mental illness and grief are, I believe, the three biggest hurdles to attain sobriety. When people first stop using, all of a sudden they come face to face with all the losses they've experienced, but never worked through because of their drinking and drug usage.

Grief is a "process," not an "event." Grief is an emotional response to some type of loss, large or small, real or imagined.

Types of Losses:

1. **Possessions**: homes, businesses, cars, trucks, etc. Two of my most prized possessions were a 1958 Willie's Wagon and a 1979 TransAm.
2. **Life Style**: I'm so grateful for my new life, but for several years into my recovery, I missed my old lifestyle. I didn't want to go to back to it, but I missed the attention of being the toughest man around and having all the good drugs, etc.
3. **Body Parts**: I hurt my knee and had an operation. Afterwards, it caused me a lot of problems and I knew I was never going to get to be the heavyweight champion of the world. I have friends who have lost eyesight, limbs, hysterectomies, etc.
4. **Dreams or Plans**: So many lost dreams. I never thought I would get divorced and not be able to live with my children. All the lost jobs. I was always able to get moved up in my job quickly and everything looking good and then get busted or drink/drug all night and not be able to get to work. I finally realized that no matter how good things were looking, I was going to screw it up.
5. **Person**: All the lost relationships. Loss of my children, my father's death, friends, etc.

Stages of Grief:

1. **Denial**: Healthy denial is a gift to not having to be totally overwhelmed by a loss like when my dad died and mom and us kids were able to follow through with our lives and work through the grief in our time. Many people get "stuck" in denial that turns into anger and/or depression, sometimes for years, even an entire lifetime.

2. **Emotional Release**: We need to learn how to identify the feelings and appropriate ways to express them. As a therapist, I constantly am asking, "How do you feel?" Pointing out simple basic feeling words like, Mad, Sad, Glad, Afraid, Hurt, Ashamed, etc. It may be very apparent to me, but the client needs to express and verbalize these feelings. That's a huge part of the process.

3. **Bargaining**: I'll go to the bar, but just drink pop. I'll just drink beer or only smoke pot. If you get me out of this God, I'll change. Maybe if I call and tell her I'll change, etc., etc.

4. **Isolation – Withdraw (it's important to be with others)**: We can physically withdraw. I have to be mindful because I can be in a large group of people and still be by myself.

5. **Acceptance**: This is the goal – to achieve acceptance. Acceptance doesn't mean that the pain necessarily goes away (it will in time), but it allows us to share the pain and experience comfort from being with others. The process that allows us to be able to feel peace amongst the pain and gradually it gets better. I'm not the only one and I don't have to be alone.

> "Do not worry about anything, but in everything by prayer and supplication with thanksgiving let your requests be known to God. And the peace of God, which surpasses all understanding will guard your hearts and your minds in Christ Jesus" (Philippians 4:6-7).

Symptoms of Grief:

When most people talk about being depressed, they are really talking about grief. Clinically diagnosed Depression is completely different. Clinical Depression isn't about loss. I have a diagnosis of chronic depression due to a chemical imbalance in my brain that I need antidepressant medications for, but we are talking about grief. These symptoms can help you detect grief, whether in yourself or others.

1. **Fatigue** – Loss of energy, low motivation
2. **Loss of Appetite** – loss of appetite is common for most people, unless you have an eating disorder.
3. **Look Older** – I've worked with many adolescents and it always amazed me how beat down and unattractive they look. However, in a relatively short time in treatment, as they work on their issues and develop hope and faith, they began to look so attractive and vitalized. Adults even more so.
4. **Comes in Waves** – If you don't remember anything else, I hope you remember this: "Grief comes in waves." When you are at that peak, feeling that you can't take it, it's too devastating, just hold on because it <u>will</u> get better and you <u>will</u> experience relief.
5. **Focus on Lost Object** - (everything reminds you of the loss)
6. **Intense Pain** - (almost prevents person from doing anything). It's very important to force yourself to eat, sleep, take a walk, etc.

Overcoming Grief:
1. **Make Sacrifice** – Giving up "Poor Me," working on the 12 Steps, pick up the 500 lb. phone, go to movie, and get involved.
2. **Stop Asking "Why"** – Facing the facts means accepting the "Reality" of the situation (loss). Someday we may understand, but not now. "Act ourselves into a new way of thinking."
3. **Sanctification** – Releasing, "Letting Go," Praying and trusting in God.
4. **Gratitude** – Looking for the Good (for death, remember and treasure the loving moments/memories).Through all sorrow /loss /trauma, we are forced to grow personally and spiritually.
5. **Releasing in Love** – We become Instruments. We learn how we can help others through our experiences. We begin to use it for good.

Helping the Healing Process:

The following is a paper I wrote almost 20 years ago about the processes I went through in my journey to healing. This paper has been very helpful over the years to many of my clients who are overwhelmed by unresolved grief:

Wounded. Grief. Time. Pain. Despair. Depression. Pain. Shock. Betrayal. Fear. Anguish. Panic. Loneliness. Hopelessness. Anger. Deep breaths. Depression. Walking! People. God. Time! Self-esteem. Worth. Prayer. Faith. Hope. Hate. Understanding. Forgiveness. Letting go. People. Comfort. Love. People. Time!!! Understanding. Forgiveness.

Remember, healing is a "process," not an event. It is not something that just happens, but instead any type of loss is a wound that requires a process we must somehow go through for healthy healing to take place. Mental wounds can take very long periods of time to completely heal, and that is fine. Don't worry about or feel bad if you end up taking a long time to heal from a loss or injustice. There is not a time limit restriction on you. Take your time, but it is important to place ourselves in the process of healing.

How do we do that? What is the process of healing? What are the steps? I believe healing is an individual journey that can be facilitated in many ways. First, I would like to compare mental healing to physical healing.

Once I hurt my knee while practicing karate kicks. For three weeks I had to keep off of it as much as possible, take a couple of aspirins, but basically I just had to give it time to heal naturally. I also started lifting weights (real light poundage) to strengthen my legs and at karate wore a leg brace for awhile. Another example is having an operation. If you follow directions, it still takes quite awhile to completely heal. It took me a good year to really heal from a serious operation. Later my father had a serious operation and I knew it would take him over a year or more to really begin to feel good.

Our bodies are made to heal themselves. It just takes time, it just takes time! If we do our part we can facilitate that healing process. So it is with mental hurts – our minds are made to heal our pain, but we also need to help facilitate healing so we can be healed more wholesomely.

Be gentle with yourself. Allow yourself time to heal. After talking with Dr. Paul Welter (Kearney State College Professor and author of several books), I began to realize we can experience grief, but not fall into deep depression. I can feel sadness from a loss, but still feel joy from a new friendship. I can feel pain, and at the same time feel happy because something special has happened for a friend. What a gift – I have to play a little slower, but I can still play!

I questioned Paul about the length of grief over a loss of a relationship. A friend of mine felt I should be over it and discounted (I felt) my feelings, but with Paul's help I was reaffirmed that healing sometimes can take a long time. Paul said that, "We're beginning to find out that healing through grief takes longer than we thought." He also suggested as part of my healing that I sit down with my friend and help him understand how deep my feelings of grief were. I did this, and it was a healing experience.

A very dear friend of mine, my sponsor Joe, talked with me about grief because he also experienced loss. I asked him especially about the loss of his first wife by death, and his second by divorce.

Joe told me that it was mainly through Step 3 of A.A., "Made a decision to turn our will and our lives over to the care of God as we understood him," (p. 59 in the 12x12) that he was able to work through it. Joe said: "I kept saying, Let Go and Let God, over and over and finally was able to let go and felt a spiritual experience, "a peace that passes all understanding," as quoted form the Bible – a surrender process. It lasted through her dying, funeral, and afterwards. I remember lying in bed crying with a smile; maybe because I knew she was okay. The key was surrendering – not fighting it. If I would have had clenched fists towards heaven, I'd have been in a lot of trouble. My A.A. training and faith helped me to Let Go. I don't recall any anger towards anyone."

The divorce, however, was a different feeling for Joe. He shared how it began with the same surrender process, but he experienced a lot of anger, resentment and hate and how he used those feelings as an aid in his healing as a way to protect himself. Calling her names and talking about his anger. Joe's ex-wife was filing for custody of their five-year-old daughter and 20 years ago it was unheard of for a father to get custody. He was very distraught about the idea of losing his youngest daughter. "The love of my life," he called her. Finally, the night before court, he was able to truly, totally give his daughter over to God. Trust that God is in charge and whatever was best for her he was okay with. Finally he became willing to lose her.

Joe said, "You know Bill, from that moment on, I was a winner. I was a winner when I went into that courtroom. They didn't know, but I knew, because I had become willing to lose everything." Then the miraculous happened and Joe was awarded custody.

Lewis Smedes in his book, "Forgive and Forget", writes about the fable of "The Magic Eyes," in which an angel tells the main character:

> "There was one remedy, he said, only one, for the hurt of a wounded heart. Fowke would need the miracle of the magic eyes. He would need eyes that could look back to the beginning of his trust and see his Hilda, not as a wife who betrayed him, but as a weak woman who needed him. Only a

new way of looking at things through the magic eyes could heal the trust flowing from the wounds of yesterday" (p. XIV)

In the book, "Love is Letting Go of Fear," Gerald Jampolsky says about the same thing when he says that we have to let go of the misperception the other person has hurt us. We have to change our perception to where we see that people are either operating out of love (positively) or out of fear (negatively). It is a process of changing my perceptions from looking at what they have done to me and realizing how hurt, angry, confused, etc. they must be to behave in such ways. I also need to look at myself and my past in such a way that I can forgive myself because I too have been mentally and spiritually very sick at times. It is trying to perceive a world where everyone is innocent and choosing to look for the love and good from the past.

But how does someone do that? How do you forgive when you have been betrayed? It is hard! According to Smedes it is done in four stages: hurt, hate, healing and coming together (p. 2). At the time of writing this paper, I got in touch with a lot of feelings of hate for my ex-fiancé – passive hate. I didn't think I hated, but I realized deep down I really didn't wish her the best. I prayed for her to have everything I wanted for myself, which is an important spiritual exercise to do, but it was through gritted teeth. That is passive hate, and I have felt a healing just by beginning to recognize that feeling and being honest with myself.

The healing is just a part of all this effort to understand, to let go, to look to God and people. How much we need others! The comfort that I can experience today from the love of certain people I've allowed into my life! Sometimes even a smile or little kindness from a perfect stranger has touched my heart and added some healing.

As you can see, my approach is spiritually-based. It's more difficult to help someone who doesn't believe in God, in spirituality. For that person it is necessary to focus on how that wound is affecting them and that they need to forgive and let go for their own peace of mind. I don't know though, because I truly rely on and believe that all healing comes through the Grace of God.

My study really doesn't touch on that aspect directly as it is basically a spiritual experience or journey that I have sought out due to my own strong spiritual beliefs and needs. Everything I have tried and the underlying motive has been part of a quest to develop a deeper sense of spirituality, because I didn't feel anything else could heal the pain so deep in my soul.

Many years ago when I was in a tremendous amount of pain, I had called home to talk with my mom, but no one was home except my youngest brother (age 18 at the time). I was sobbing, feeling absolute pain and despair. Dick said to take some deep breaths and calm down, just slow down. That was a major beginning of some healing for me. I constantly reminded myself to take a deep breath and let go of everything for five minutes at a time, then I moved that up the next day to ten minutes at a time, and so on. It worked. I was able to walk through the pain by slowing down and reaching out to God and people.

I went to an "Inner Healing Retreat" conducted in Concordia, Kansas, by Father Jim Schmidt, which I felt was very beneficial. Father Jim started out by quoting from the Bible, Thessalonians, Chapter 5, verses 16-18:

> **"Always be joyful. Always keep on praying.**
> **No matter what happens, always be thankful,**
> **for this is God's will for you who belong to**
> **Christ Jesus."**

He said tell me how grateful you are and I'll tell you how healed you are. And for Jim, "inner healing" means getting to the point where you can say, "It really doesn't matter."

Father Jim stressed the importance of getting in touch with God, being a God of love and that He is right here with us. He comes down to us and actually lives with us and within us. "God happens to us."

The beginning of "inner healing" is discovering our giftedness, and Jim quoted from the Bible, Isaiah 43:

> **"Fear not ... because you are precious in my**
> **eyes and glorious and because I love you."**

Self esteem is a part of this, and he pointed out some key suggestions to develop self-esteem:

1. Live consciously, beware and take responsibility
2. Live independently. If you're a "plum" be the best plum you can be. Don't try to be a "peach." Some people don't like plums and that is okay.
3. Willingness to take responsibility for my own existence. Jimmy Williams said in his A.A. talk, and his words come through my mind quite often, "It's never them. It is never the people or the situation that needs to change. It is always me, it's never them." It would be nice if people or situations would change, but that is not under my control.
4. Honest and straight-forward about our feelings. Keep around people who love me and respect me. Sponsor Joe said there are two kinds of people: Chicken Soup People and Chicken Shit People.
5. Integrity – being accountable and responsible and have the humility to be honest with who we are.
6. Live productively – doing our best and recognizing our weaknesses and strengths.

So the beginning of "Inner Healing" is first discovering our giftedness; second, healing through positive memories; and third, healing through negative memories.

Healing through positive memories is looking for God working in our lives. "In times of desolation go back and look at the times of consolations." Healing through negative memories involves allowing ourselves to see things differently. Quoting Jim, "It's what I <u>think</u> about the <u>events</u> that causes what I <u>feel</u>." Jampolsky, in his book, "Love is Letting Go of Fear," which I had mentioned earlier, talked about the same thing. We can't change what happened, but we can change our perceptions which can help heal our feelings.

Guided imagery, meditation and prayer are very healing actions. I've also used different forms of Gestalt therapy techniques which have been very helpful.

I went to my room and placed two chairs so they faced each other. Sitting in one, I asked God to sit down with me. I wrote down in my journal the conversation:

Date: 9-20-86

<u>Bill:</u>   God, I've been hurting and struggling for a long time – ever since I've been sober and before. I feel a lot of anger. I don't like it, and don't want to feel that way. I also feel a lot of real hurt and loneliness.

I'm angry at you because I prayed for your help with Erin and me; and even though I prayed for Your will I wanted you to keep us together. I see people all around getting married, starting lives together and I want that so bad, so much. I just miss Erin and Sean so much. And I am real damn angry at Erin to walk away from me for the second time, for being so dishonest, and for treating me so cruelly. And it hurts, so much, that she'd do that.

It is so completely powerless to me because she started using (drinking), and I want to go get drunk and show them all. I'm so tired; I feel the natural needs for sex and love, but even more intensely.

The last thing I'm angry or disappointed about is how distant You seem to be from me, and maybe I ask for too much, but You say in Your Holy Word to come to You as little children. God, here I am – please help me to hear and feel you because I can't do it by my weak little self.

<u>God:</u>   Bill, be still, just be still. I don't like you being angry at me, and I know you are hurting.

Then I spoke to Erin about my grief also.

<u>Erin:</u>   Bill, I'm sorry – I love you a lot. I just had to grow. I have a lot of growing to do and it's painful. Pray for me will you please, and forgive me. I miss you.

<u>Bill:</u>   Erin, Erin, Erin, I miss you, and I miss your son. I know you have a lot of growing to do and I do also, but I wish we could have done it together. I hate it that our love has caused us so much pain. Or maybe it was only me that loved deeply.

<u>Bill:</u>   God, I accept that you don't want to talk to me at this moment, but I need to ask you for your Grace so that I can enter into forgiveness. The grace to forgive you, to forgive Erin, to forgive dad, and forgive Ernie, to forgive the world, to forgive Ann, to forgive the adolescent staff. Also, the Grace to get in touch with my feelings toward self and the

grace to forgive myself too. Actually I do feel proud of myself for trying so hard and continuing on one day at a time for almost eight years. I have been changed a lot and am grateful for the Grace to have stayed sober and straight. God, it has been painful.

I cried a little just now, as I read through that journal and wrote it out; but, I guess that is part of the healing process.

The Linn brothers, Dennis and Matthew, in their book, "Healing Life's Hurts," point out the five stages of healing a memory:

<u>Stages In Healing a Memory</u>

Denial	I don't admit I was ever hurt
Anger	I blame others for hurting and destroying me
Bargaining	I set up conditions before I'm ready to forgive
Depression	I blame myself for letting hurt destroy me
Acceptance	I look forward to growth from hurt

So these are the stages that I've described previously that we need to work through in our healing, and some exercises can help to lead us through these stages. According to the Linn brothers, we need to work through these stages with Christ and friends. We need to share continually our feelings, whatever they are, with God and friends.

My favorite professor, Kent Estes, always said, you deal with a problem by jumping into the middle of it and seeing what's there, which is breaking through the denial stage. Many of the exercises Father Jim talked about are tools to help us to take responsibility for our feelings so that our self worth is not tied up to how someone else treats us or to what circumstances of life we find ourselves. Working through anger towards forgiveness, but the first step is getting in touch with whatever feelings we are experiencing and this can only happen through sharing with God and others.

The goal is acceptance, acceptance of whatever the situation. In this stage is doesn't mean that the pain has gone away, but it does mean we don't have to be alone anymore. We can experience some peace and comfort amongst the pain and with time the pain will subside. And hopefully we will reach that place which Father Jim shared when we can say, "It doesn't really matter," somehow "it's okay."

Victor Frankl, in his book, "Man's Search for Meaning" quoted Nietzsche, "He who has a 'why' to live for, can bear with almost any 'how'" (p. 97), which is at the core of Frankl's philosophy that man needs to search for and find a meaning for life. When he was in the concentration camps he said, "We had to learn ourselves, and furthermore, we had to teach the despairing men, that it did not really matter what we expected from life, but rather what life expected from us" (p. 98). So if suffering happens to be what is expected of us at times then we are responsible, or more importantly we need to find out the meaning for us in that suffering. "When we are no longer able to change a situation – just think of an incurable disease such as inoperable cancer – we are challenged to change ourselves" (p. 135).

One other thought that Frankl pointed out is that possibly because of our value system when we find ourselves feeling unhappy/depressed, we not only feel unhappy, but also ashamed for feeling that way (p. 137). It is so important to be gentle with ourselves and with others, but I think it is even harder to be gentle with ourselves.

Helping the healing process! Time, time, time. Reaching out to God and others. As simple as taking deep breaths five minutes at a time. At times, grief can be so absolutely devastating that it feels like there is nothing else, but from my own personal experience God was there with me and HE is there with you. He happens to us! Sometimes it is just a matter of having to sit there and hurt. Quit fighting the reality, because it just makes us more exhausted. Just begin walking through the pain – one foot in front of the other. Actually going for walks is very helpful – just the action of forcing yourself to put one foot in front of the other is helpful. Use this time to pray while walking.

And forgiveness seems to be the key, but from my experience this can ultimately come only through the Grace of God.

The Linn brothers quoted from the Bible, Luke 6, verses 27 and 28, "Love your enemies. Do good to those who hate you. Pray for the happiness of those who curse you; implore God's blessing on those who hurt you.

I would like to end this paper with a story Father Jerome Rausch (Crosier Monastery) shared with me when I reached out to him for help. At first, it didn't seem very meaningful, but it grows on you, and I believe it talks about Faith.

Good News, Bad News

An old Austrian farmer bought a horse that was
by far the best in the county. Not even the King
had a better horse. The farmer's neighbor came
by and said, "Wow, are you lucky to have that
horse." The farmer said, "Well, who knows,
good luck, bad luck, who knows."
A couple of weeks later the horse broke out of the
corral and ran away to join up with some
wild horses. The neighbor dropped by and said,
"Oh, what bad luck, bad luck, that's terrible."
But the farmer said, "Good luck, bad luck,
how can you tell?"
A week later the horse came back and brought
with it three wild mares that were also
very, very good stock. When the neighbor found
this out he said, "I can't believe it,
what tremendously good luck to not only
get your horse back, but get three mares also."
The farmer said, "Who knows, good luck, bad
luck, who knows."
Later, Darp, the farmer's son was breaking the
new horses when he was thrown and broke
his leg badly, and had to be in a big cast.
The neighbor said, "Oh, that's terrible, what
terrible bad luck. I am so sorry for your son and
you." But the farmer said, "Who knows,
good luck, bad luck, how do you know?"
A terrible war started and the army came through
making every young man join up and go to the front
lines, which was almost certain death. But the farmer's
son couldn't go because of his broken leg.
Good luck, bad luck. Who knows?
How can you tell?

Father Jim said, "Where you stumble and fall and get knocked down in life, that is where you find gold." A dual question we were asked at the Inner Healing Retreat was:

When was the time you felt the biggest loss?

When was the time you felt the closest to God?

These experiences have the power to drop us into total desolation or into a powerful spiritual experience.

CHAPTER 32

15 MINUTES A DAY

**YOU'RE
READING
THE
PROOF
THIS
TECHNIQUE
WORKS**

**I WOKE UP EARLY THIS MORNING
AND PAUSED BEFORE
ENTERING THE DAY.
I HAD SO MUCH
TO ACCOMPLISH,
I HAD TO TAKE TIME TO
PRAY.**

In November of 1978, I read an article in Guideposts Magazine titled, "Just 15 Minutes a Day" and that short article has made a tremendous difference in my life.

The author, Charlotte Hale Allen, asks which dreams I'd like to accomplish, and challenges me that many of these could be accomplished in just 15 minutes a day. Since I was just learning to live life one day at a time, an hour, or minute at a time, I was open to this concept.

I want to pass this little jewel of a concept on to you, and know you will be amazed also. This idea has helped me hundreds of times to do things I wasn't too keen on doing, and to be motivated to do activities I kept putting off. No matter how difficult a job, I could stay with it for 15 minutes.

JUST 15 MINUTES A DAY
By Charlotte Hale Allen

"What's the biggest dream of your life? How important is it? How much would you give up to make it happen? Let me pass along to you one of the most powerfully creative facts that anyone ever taught me and it's astoundingly true. You can do just about anything you want to do, if you spend just 15 minutes a day at it.

Consider this: In three years you can become an expert on any subject you care to study – Chinese art, computer programming, cooking, chess, bridge, bricklaying, anything – if you work at it 15 minutes a day.

In just one year or less you can accomplish some tremendous tasks by investing about 15 minutes a day. For example, you could:

1. Read the entire Bible
2. Plant and keep a small garden
3. Become physically fit
4. Learn to play a musical instrument
5. Paint a house
6. Learn a foreign language
7. Write a book

Remembering the day I discovered the magic of 15 minutes still makes me smile. My husband and I had driven to a small town in the country that hot summer Saturday, to call on a friend who was the town's only doctor, an ardent do-it-yourselfer. He'd recently bought a sprawling Victorian house and we discovered him sitting in the middle of a room, surrounded by paint cans and a clutter of tools, gazing toward the ceiling and muttering, "That thing's gotta come down!"

We thought he'd flipped – especially when we learned that George intended to repair, repaint or refurnish every room in that three-story monstrosity by himself.

How long would it take? Where would he find the time? How unrealistic could he get?

A quick tour of the already-completed rooms, however, aroused our interest and excitement. I admired a charming "new" bathroom in which George had lowered the ceiling, installed and painted new storage cabinets, hung wallpaper, changed light fixtures, and even provided heated towel bars.

"I work fifteen minutes at a time, but never stop before my time is up," George explained. "That's the secret: Work fifteen minutes a day, without fail."

Still, I was skeptical. I couldn't believe such a simple plan could possibly help me. I decided to give it a try.

That was more than 20 years ago and since then I've had great fun with those magic chunks of time. My first project was to tackle a badly neglected flower garden which was choked with weeds. Every time I looked out the dining room window, I fretted, because I thought I had no time whatever to try to redeem that impossible garden.

That's when I learned how many weeds I could pull in 15 minutes! It took just one week, snatching a quarter hour here, another there, to get that flower border tidy and ready for new transplants.

The beauty of 15 minutes a day is that it helps me to stop postponing those things I really want or need to do and get them under way. It banishes discouragement and halts procrastination. The method works on any job or goal that matters to me, whether it's writing a book or cleaning all the kitchen cupboards.

Many grim little jobs really don't deserve more than 15 minutes a day, anyhow. Done all at once, they'd be too much of a bad thing. You know the jobs I mean: filing papers, cleaning closets, polishing silver, tidying a garage or tool shed."

What are some things you've been putting off doing? When we put off something that needs our attention, it's a double loss. We deprive ourselves in two ways: first we feel bad for putting it off, "procrastination," and secondly, which is something I didn't realize, is you miss out on the positive, wonderful feelings that come from accomplishing a goal.

I painted my house and trim and took one window/door at a time. It looks great! I have to stop in my driveway coming in and going out, just to look at it. I stained my deck. I cleaned the garage. I'm back at school for computers, taking one class at a time.

This concept has helped hundreds of my clients to go back to school, work the 12-Step program, complete assignments, restore relationships and walk themselves back into a productive life.

Just 15 minutes a day equals out to 91 hours per year. That amounts to two 45 hour work weeks!

Think what you could do with two extra weeks to do whatever you want but haven't had time. It's there for you and it's not even a sacrifice, just a magical feel good time!

So seriously, what goals, dreams and plans would you like to accomplish? Let this be your first "15 minutes" to take the time to write out this list. It's really an amazing tool. Pick it up and begin using it.

I wanted to read the Bible from cover to cover, but that looked like too much, so I made a commitment to just read it daily for 15 minutes. I've read it twice now, in addition to my morning meditations. No matter how busy I am, I can take 15 minutes.

Nowhere has this helped me more than in my relationship with God. I almost always spend more time in prayer and meditation, but 15 minutes a day is such a great tool to get me started. It is absolutely necessary to begin my day with getting in touch with God and aligning my will to God's will. Whenever I'm frustrated, impatient, angry, etc., that's usually (always) the problem.

When I was promoted to maintenance man in 1979, the shop was a total disaster. Junk, bolts, screws, washers, nuts and nails were in several big boxes and stuff was everywhere. I did my maintenance work but forced myself to begin separating everything for at least 15 minutes every day. It took several months, but that shop looked good.

If, due to injury or illness I got out of the habit of working out, it was difficult to get started again. I felt too tired and swore I'd start tomorrow. I had lots of excuses, but anyone can do a couple of exercises for just 15 minutes a day, and pretty soon I'd be back on track, working out, feeling great.

When I was going to school, I kept it simple and just studied a little bit daily. Of course, once you get started with school and developing better study habits, you can study much harder. I love going to school and learning.

While writing this book, Lent came up, so I'd given up the usual candies and desserts, but I wanted to do more. I prayed, asking God for guidance. The idea was to force myself to write for at least 30 minutes or more every night. Then the rough draft of this book was finished. Then the editing of this book, just a few pages at a time. Eventually, almost unbelievably, this book was completed.

This ties back in with the Master Key to Riches philosophy that when we look at the difficulties of a situation, we become overwhelmed before even getting started. When I started treatment centers, I couldn't look at the whole job; it was too enormous. I just took it step by step, trusting in God and this process. This idea works and I hope you'll let it work for you also.

Something that might help you is developing a 15 minute commitment contract to help you reach your goals. The contract might look something like this:

<u>My "15 MINUTE" Personal Commitment/Contract</u>

What are my long-term goals/dreams?

     1.

     2.

     3.

What are my short-term goals/dreams?

     1.

     2.

     3.

What would I like to do 15 minutes a day?

     1.

     2.

     3.

I _____ **am making a personal**

commitment to do _____

_____ **15 minutes a day**

until I accomplish _____**.**

Signed:_____

CONGRATULATIONS!

A poem that has made a huge difference to me is titled, "The Difference":

THE DIFFERENCE

I GOT UP EARLY ONE MORNING
AND RUSHED RIGHT INTO THE DAY;
I HAD SO MUCH TO ACCOMPLISH
THAT I DIDN'T HAVE TIME TO PRAY.
PROBLEMS JUST TUMBLED AROUND ME
AND HEAVIER CAME EACH TASK;
'WHY DOESN'T GOD HELP ME?'
I WONDERED.
HE SAID,
'BUT YOU DIDN'T ASK.'
I WANTED TO SEE JOY AND BEAUTY
BUT THE DAY TOILED ON,
GRAY AND BLEAK;
I WONDERED WHY GOD
DIDN'T SHOW ME.
HE SAID,
'BUT YOU DIDN'T SEEK.'
I TRIED TO COME INTO GOD'S
PRESENCE;
I USED ALL MY KEYS AT THE LOCK.
GOD GENTLY AND LOVINGLY CHIDED,
'MY CHILD, YOU DIDN'T KNOCK.'
I WOKE UP EARLY THIS MORNING
AND PAUSED BEFORE
ENTERING THE DAY.
I HAD SO MUCH TO ACCOMPLISH
THAT I HAD TO TAKE TIME TO PRAY.

CHAPTER 33

RELAXATION/ MEDITATION/ SELF-HYPNOSIS

**"IF
WE
KEEP DOING
THE SAME THINGS
OVER
AND
OVER,
WE'RE
GOING TO
KEEP GETTING
THE SAME
RESULTS
OVER
AND
OVER."**

Other than prayer, I believe learning to relax is the most important ingredient in a healthy lifestyle. I've spent several years studying different ways to meditate. I'm also a certified hypnotist and all I've learned continues to point to the importance of relaxing and going into a meditation state that ends with simple self hypnosis (positive self talk).

The science of hypnosis is actually one of the earliest sciences, dating before Christ. Way back in time before all the medicines we have today, people understood the power of the mind. I think we've lost some of that knowledge over the years, but it is now beginning to resurface.

Our minds are very powerful, but we have to do the work, the mental exercises. It's the same as working out with weights. If I'm going to gain strength and look good, I have to do the exercises regularly. The discipline I learned from weightlifting has translated into this area also.

Of course I want to be lazy, or am too busy to take the time, or I procrastinate, so I really have to make commitments and let my support system know I need to stay on task.

Whenever we are upset, frustrated, angry, hyper, fearful, etc., the first step to calming down is <u>always</u> taking deep breaths. We cannot slow our minds down until we slow our body down. So we have to take deep breaths and exhale slowly, concentrating only on breathing. Once we accomplish deep breathing, then we can place our attention on our minds and our thinking. I'll take you through a very good relaxation exercise after I finish a few points.

When we enter into this relaxed state of body and mind, we can also do some very simple, but life changing, self-hypnosis scripts.

Hypnosis is a process to bypass our conscious minds and go deep into our subconscious minds. A very simple example of the separateness of conscious and subconscious mind is, for example, when you are talking to someone and you want to remember something and you say, "Wait a minute, let me think and remember this." At that exact moment, you are going from your conscious mind to your subconscious mind.

Our conscious mind is very critical and doesn't allow anything to enter that doesn't agree with your belief system. This can be very negative if we have erroneous beliefs. The conscious mind has short-term memory.

Our subconscious minds store all the long-term memory, including all the trauma we've experienced, and sometimes negative beliefs which have guided our lives. No wonder that, at times, we keep experiencing the same problems over and over.

A wise old adage:

**"IF WE KEEP DOING
THE SAME THINGS
OVER AND OVER,
WE'RE GOING TO
KEEP GETTING
THE SAME RESULTS
OVER AND OVER."**

If we don't like the results or consequences, then we'd better stop to see what needs to change. When we identify dysfunctional beliefs, then we can use self-hypnosis to strengthen our new positive functional beliefs. This is an inside job – real inside, because in fact it's our subconscious thoughts that need to be changed.

I've made several relaxation, meditative hypnotic tapes that can be purchased, or you can make your own, but you have to listen to them on a daily basis, or even twice a day for the most benefit.

With these tapes, what I do is to lull the conscious mind into letting its guard down so I can talk directly to your subconscious mind. Or, if you make your own tapes, you can talk directly to your subconscious mind. This allows for very deep effective change to take place and that is really what hypnosis is all about. On the following page is a Self-Hypnosis script. I suggest that once a day, or at night, you set aside 15 minutes to relax and go into a hypnotic state and just relax and be open to becoming more positive and trusting.

Remember that the only people this won't work for are the ones who don't believe or trust. If you are willing, you will experience the benefits.

A RELAXING MEDITATIVE SELF-HYPNOSIS SCRIPT

Please sit or lie down comfortably and I ask that you find a spot on the wall a little above eye level and concentrate, looking at it and even through it. At the same time I would like you to begin taking deep breaths, breathing in deeply, exhaling slowly. As you breathe in, breath in the freshness of new life, oxygen, God's spirit and as you exhale allow all the tensions to flow out. As your eyes begin to feel tired and heavy, allow yourself to relax more deeply. Your eyelids are now very heavy, so allow your eyes to close.

If you have any problems, for the time being I ask that you pack them into an imaginary briefcase or suitcase and place it down on the floor next to you. At the end of this exercise you can pick it back up or leave it and walk away, but for right now, you are problem free.

I would like you to imagine a beautiful golden ball of energy that looks like the sun, but it's not hot and it's hovering right over your head. The energizing, vitalizing rays feel incredibly wonderful. Allow those wonderful soothing rays to enter through the top of your head, totally relaxing all the cells and fibers of your brain. You feel so very relaxed. Allow the rays to flow down into your temples, down into your eyes and jaws, leaving just a wonderful, soothing, energized feeling. Allow the golden rays of healing energy to relax all of your facial muscles.

Now allow the relaxing golden rays to travel down into your neck and shoulders as you feel all the tension flow down your body. Let the relaxing rays relax your arms, biceps, forearms and fingers. Allow the relaxing feeling to enter into your back, lower back, down into your legs. The total relaxation continues traveling downward through all your muscles, into your legs, thighs, calves, feet and down through your toes.

Just enjoy this feeling of total relaxation and realize how good it feels just to be relaxed. So often we're so busy we forget to just stop and enjoy feeling relaxed, trusting that everything is okay.

Now that you are totally relaxed, I am going to say some things directly to your subconscious mind. I won't say anything harmful, but only positive messages. These positive messages will replace any old negative messages you may have received, even those possibly received all the way back to childhood.

You are open to these messages because you want to be happy and feel more energy. You are now in a deep hypnotic rest. You are very, very deeply relaxed and you realize that you are quite capable of repeating this exercise whenever you find yourself anxious or frustrated. When you do, you will feel calm, peaceful and energized.

Because of this deep, relaxing rest, you will feel stronger and more fit in every way. You will be more alert and discover your thinking is very clear and your memory much improved.

When you awake, you will feel very energetic. You will feel very positive about yourself and will realize that you are a very capable person. Instead of feeling discouraged, you will feel very encouraged. Your thinking will become much clearer and you will be more interested in whatever task you have to perform. Your mind will become completely distracted away from yourself. You will think more about what you can do for others and experience a greater joy because you no longer dwell on your problems and difficulties. In fact, when you do think of your difficulties, you will feel excited about the possibilities. You will be much less pre-occupied with yourself and how you feel. You will constantly think of all the many things to be grateful for and always see the positive in every situation. You will accept these suggestions because this is what you want and this is good for you.

When you awake, you will be able to concentrate more easily, think more clearly and see things in their true perspective. You will realize that you can deal with anything and have a greater belief in God. You will experience a deeper faith and allow yourself to feel, in a much more meaningful way, the power of God's grace.

In a couple of minutes, you will count from five to one and upon saying one you will wake up, feeling wonderful, refreshed and excited to be alive. Every time you do this exercise, you will go deeper into a hypnotic rest state. All of this will happen because that is what you want and is good for you.

Now count: 5 – beginning to emerge, 4 – coming back, 3 – feeling more alert, 2 – wakening up feeling great and 1 – wide awake, feeling refreshed, excited and better than ever.

How did that feel? It felt great! I know it felt wonderful because it's what we all want and we just need to be reprogrammed at a deeper level. This may be your first experience of the wonderful benefits of this hypnotic experience. Keep at it and you'll find yourself feeling better and better.

CHAPTER 34

A JOURNEY YOU DON'T WANT TO MISS

"MY FAVORITE PROFESSOR
AND VERY GOOD FRIEND,
DR. KENT ESTES'
FAVORITE
SAYING:
'BE KIND
TO EVERYONE
YOU MEET,
BECAUSE WE ARE
ALL FIGHTING
A TOUGH BATTLE
AT DIFFERENT TIMES
OF OUR LIVES.'"

Note: My friend, Dr. Kent Preston Estes, died on 1-13-05 from cancer and is greatly missed.

"As you face your death it is only the love you've given and received which will count." This quote guided Kent's life.

"I have fought the good fight, I have finished the race, I have kept the faith. 2 Timothy 4:7

It's been an impossible journey, way beyond my capabilities. Life is a journey beyond any of our capabilities. It's that way purposely so that we can open our heart to God. None of us is going to get out of this life alive!

I hope this book will help the reader learn from life and see the value in every experience.

Over the years, my life has been very, very difficult. Besides the severe mental breakdown, I've also had to turn myself into a psychiatric hospital twice. Both times were horrendous and I was frightened that I wouldn't get better. Thank God I did, after some medication adjustments and mental health therapy.

Sometimes it's frightening to realize how delicate our brain chemistry is. Just a little imbalance can cause immense mental pain and anguish.

My favorite professor and very good friend, Dr. Kent Estes, had a favorite saying:

> ## "BE KIND TO EVERYONE YOU MEET, BECAUSE WE ARE ALL FIGHTING A TOUGH BATTLE AT DIFFERENT TIMES IN OUR LIVES."

Be kind, be gentle with everyone, and especially ourselves, or we won't be able or have it to give.

When you mix the insanity of the alcohol/addict with medical/chemical imbalance, it can be devastating. The good news is that anyone can get better if they ask God for help and follow His guidance to the people and programs that can help.

This reminds me of a story of a man who was caught in a flood. The water had risen up to his roof and he desperately prayed to God for help. A rowboat came by and offered to let him in, but he said, "No, God is going to save me." Soon a raft came by, the water was still rising, and they asked the man if he wanted to climb in. But he said, "No, God is going to save me." Finally the water rose so high he drowned. When he went to heaven and asked God why He didn't save him, God said, "I sent you a rowboat and a raft."

The moral of this story is to accept the help you're guided to.

Besides all that, just everyday life problems can be traumatic. When I first got sober, was divorced and wasn't able to be around my children, those events caused physical, mental and spiritual problems for me that required healing. I also experienced a second marriage and a couple of relationships that didn't work out. My father's death and that of my sponsor, Joe, hit hard. We all experience difficulties at times. With God's help, we can walk through everything.

My mother gave me a plaque once and a client painted a small picture that says the same thing:

> I BELIEVE
> IN THE SUN
> EVEN WHEN
> IT IS NOT SHINING.
> I BELIEVE IN LOVE
> EVEN WHEN
> I FEEL IT NOT.
> I BELIEVE IN GOD
> EVEN WHEN
> HE IS SILENT.

    This is a wonderful journey when we learn to love and feel love. We must realize it's not a do-it-yourself deal and we let God and family and friends travel together with us.

    When I've gotten stuck, confused, and wonder where God is, I sometimes read my Broken Dreams Card.

BROKEN DREAMS

AS CHILDREN BRING THEIR
BROKEN TOYS
WITH TEARS FOR US TO MEND
I BROUGHT MY BROKEN DREAMS
TO GOD
BECAUSE HE WAS MY FRIEND.
BUT THEN INSTEAD OF LEAVING HIM
IN PEACE TO WORK ALONE,
I HUNG AROUND AND TRIED TO HELP
WITH WAYS THAT WERE MY OWN.
AT LAST I SNATCHED THEM BACK
AND CRIED,
"HOW CAN YOU BE SO SLOW?"
"MY CHILD," HE SAID,
"WHAT COULD I DO?"
"YOU NEVER DID LET THEM GO."

So let's all make this journey together, regardless of race, nationality, gender, young or old, rich or poor, education or not, regardless of religious preferences, let's just do like Dr. Kent Estes said: "Be kind to everyone you meet, because we're all fighting a tough battle."

At every wedding, I always give a present with one of my favorite Bible quotes:

> **"Love is very patient and kind.**
> **It is not jealous or envious,**
> **Never boastful or proud,**
> **Never haughty or selfish or rude.**
> **Love does not demand its own way.**
> **It is not irritable or touchy. It does not hold**
> **grudges and will hardly even notice when**
> **others do it wrong. It is never glad about**
> **injustice, but rejoices whenever truth wins**
> **out. If you love someone you will be loyal to**
> **him no matter what the cost. You will always**
> **believe in him, always expect the best of him,**
> **and always stand your ground in defending**
> **him. All the special gifts and powers from**
> **God will someday come to an end,**
> **but love goes on forever.**
>
> **(I Corinthians 13, verses 4-9)**

Every Friday morning at the Siena/Francis House, we have our breakfast and community meeting. This is always a very powerful, spiritual and moving meeting. The counselors and staff always laugh about how powerful this meeting is. This meeting is where we celebrate the "MIRACLES" Addiction Recovery Program's graduations and also acknowledge all the sobriety birthdays. We also celebrate birth birthdays.

When you experience 80-90 men and women, mostly homeless, hopeless addicts/alcoholics, sitting around looking good and feeling happy, believe me, that is spiritual. Most of the time we also have family members there with eyes filled with joyful tears and gratitude and hope in their hearts to have their loved ones back.

We start out this meeting with the St. Francis Prayer, which is also the 11th Step Prayer. And, even though I have quoted it previously, it is such a powerful prayer that it is the one with which I am going to end this book.

> ## PRAYER OF ST. FRANCIS OF ASSISI
>
> **Lord, make me an instrument of your peace.**
> **Where there is hatred . . . let me sow love.**
> **Where there is injury . . . pardon.**
> **Where there is doubt . . . faith.**
> **Where there is despair . . .hope.**
> **Where there is darkness . . . light.**
> **Where there is sadness . . .joy.**
> **Divine Master,**
> **grant that I may not so much seek**
> **To be consoled . . .as to console.**
> **To be understood . . .as to understand.**
> **To be loved . . . as to love.**
> **For it is in giving . . .that we receive.**
> **It is in pardoning, that we are pardoned.**
> **It is in dying . . .that we are born**
> **to eternal life.**

The world of human suffering unceasingly calls not just for our prayers, not just our faith, but also for our love, displayed by our actions. Let's all join together to make this a better world by being instruments for God and servants to man. God bless you!

You are the world's light – a city on a hill, glowing in the night for all to see. Don't hide your light. Let it shine for all. Let your good deeds glow for all to see, so that they will praise your heavenly Father (Matthew 5:14-16).

REFERENCES

A.A. World Wide Services. (2001, 4th Edition). *Alcoholics Anonymous.* New York City.

A.A. World Wide Services (1953). *Twelve Steps and Twelve Traditions.* New York City.

Allen, Charlotte Hale. (1978). *Fifteen Minutes a Day.* Guideposts Magazine. Guideposts, Inc. Carmel, NY.

Dufford, Robert, S.J. and North American Liturgy Resources. (1975). *Be Not Afraid.*

Eppley Treatment Center. (1978). *A Guide to a Personal Moral Inventory.*

Frankl, Victor. (2000). *Man's Search for Meaning.* New York: Beacon Press.

Hazelden. (1996). *24 Hours a Day.*

Hazelden. (1998, 2nd edition). *Day by Day.*

Hill, Napoleon. (1997) *Master Key to Riches.* New York: Ballantine Books.

Jampolsky, Gerald. (1988). *Love is Letting Go of Fear.* New York: Celestial Arts.

Linn, Dennis and Matthew. (1977). *Healing Life's Hurts.* New York: Paulist Press.

Methodist Hospital. (1978). *A Guide to a Personal Moral Inventory.* Eppley Treatment Center

National Recovery Network. Telephone: (402)477-2372. E-mail address: nebraskarecovery@prodigy.net.

Smedes, Lewis. (1996). *Forgive and Forget.* San Francisco: Harper.

INDEX
4TH AND 5TH STEP INVENTORY GUIDE

A personal moral inventory is our opportunity to be honest about ourselves. It is a very important step in the recovery process. In this step we demonstrate our willingness to search through the rubble of our lives, to fearlessly look at our behavior and become acutely aware of how that behavior has been harmful and destruction to us and to others. This should be done in a non-judgmental way. There is no need to play judge, jury and executioner. Simply look at the behavior and let it speak for itself. It can help us become aware of how our intentions and our behavior are all too often inconsistent.

Through this process we are able to examine our personal, moral values. How have we violated these values? How have we "gone against" our sense of "right" and "wrong." What behavior isolates us from others and ourselves? What have we done that ultimately ends in loneliness and feelings of brokenness, wretchedness and despair?

In this Guide to a Personal Moral Inventory, we are also encouraged to examine how we are presently working the A.A. Program. This is not a balance sheet to weigh our assets against our liabilities, rather it is yet another phase in becoming honest about ourselves, our behavior, and our feelings. It is an opportunity to become aware of our moral values and ways we carry these values out.

This inventory assists us in recognizing how our behavior affects us and others. It can help us get in touch with our feelings toward ourselves and our behavior. And through this fearless searching, we may become more attuned to what the first step of A.A. has to say about our powerlessness and unmanageability.

The 4th Step of A.A.

"Made a searching and fearless moral inventory of ourselves."

The 5th Step of A.A.

"Admitted to God, to ourselves and to another human being the exact nature of our wrongs."

Here are a few guidelines that you may find helpful in making your Personal Inventory:

1. **The inventory is not a test!** Be careful you do not try to manage what someone else knows about you. The inventory is for your benefit. It is an opportunity for you to take a good look at what has been going on in your life and your part in that.
2. The following suggestions may be helpful as you write each of your examples:

a) **Focus on your behavior.** Do not justify, rationalize or take someone else's inventory. Do not ask **why** you did something; only "**what** was my behavior?" Remember, behavior is all we can change, so it is important that we examine what we do.
b) **Be specific.** Write your examples in a manner so you have no doubt that it is only **your** behavior that you are describing and could not be applicable to anyone else.
c) **Be concrete.** Describe actual experiences of yours (particular instances), not something made up or a general statement. Share a "for instance."
d) **Be honest.** Honesty is at the heart of your willingness to change. If you are not honest, it will only affect the way **you** will live **your life**.

3. Write the inventory down in such a way that you can share all the incidents during your 5th Step. This is a chance to know and surrender "The exact nature of our wrongs," and to feel the serenity and peace, and the freedom of a new life.
There are two main parts to this Guide:

A. Liabilities: our negative, destructive behavior.
   1. Defective characteristics
   2. Life relationships
   3. Ten Commandments

B. Assets: our positive, constructive behavior, recovery in action.
1. New life qualities
2. Everyday life experiences
3. Attitudes
4. Responsibilities
5. Plan for recovery

A. **Liabilities:** Our negative, destructive behavior. In this first part, search back as far as you can, as well as into the present. Fearlessly examine all your behavior. Do not limit your examples only to drinking/using behavior.

I. **Defective Characteristics:** In this section, describe the behavior that **you** and **others** are not pleased with. These are things you have done or do that you feel ashamed about or that have caused discomfort and isolation.

1) **Selfish and Self-Centeredness:** "I want what I want when I want it, no matter who has to pay the price." This is wanting to be the center of attention or feeling that everything should revolve around my wishes. Think about all the time and energy you spend trying to make sure things work out the way you want them to. In putting your own wants first, how have you hurt others and yourself?
2) **Dishonesty.** There are many ways to be dishonest. Making alibis, flat our lying, thinking dishonestly, dreaming and believing the dreams, and rationalizing in our minds. Give examples of how this deception has been part of your life.
3) **False Pride:** Thinking that I'm better or tougher than what I am is one kind of false pride. Having trouble admitting any human weakness and trying to cover up with grandiose words and behavior is yet another. How has your false pride kept you from facing the real you?
4) **Resentments:** When things don't come out the way I expect them to or the way I want them to, I feel hurt and act our my hurt in angry ways. I blame others, I hang on to angry feelings and often take those feelings out on others. Resents become good

excuses for not taking responsibility for our own feelings. What resents are you, or have you been hanging on to?

5) **Being Phony.** "I'm sure people wouldn't like me if they knew what I am really like." So I work very hard at being what I believe they would want me to be. I become a people pleasure, paying people off with false compliments or gifts, telling them what I think they want to hear. Give examples of your being phony.

6) **Being Overly Sensitive:** My feelings are often hurt very easily, especially when I believe someone is disapproving of me or the way I do something. Sometimes we get upset when we imagine that people re talking about us and "picking" on us. How have you been overly sensitive?

7) **Fear:** Being afraid of being hurt, shamed, rejected or a failure is often a terrifying experience. Sometimes we are unable to identify exactly what it is that we are afraid of, yet we feel that nothing will work out well. How have fears paralyzed or destroyed your ability to act in a confident manner?

8) **Self Pity:** Instead of admitting we are feeling sorry for ourselves, how often have we said, "I'm just a little depressed?" We may not feel understood or loved or respected and then feel sorry for ourselves, a victim of circumstances. How has self pity been a part of your behavior?

9) **Perfectionism:** Often I expect that I must do everything perfect. Sometimes I do nothing out of fear that I won't measure up to my unreal expectations. Sometimes we expect the same kind of perfection from others. How has this characteristic been evident in your life?

10) **Putting Things Off:** Waiting to get in the mood to do things often leads to never getting the job done. When someone reminds us of our irresponsible behavior, we tend to react by becoming hard to get along with: resentful. What are some things you have put off doing and the feelings you had when the pressure was put on you to get the job done?

11) **Intolerance:** When I can't accept something that doesn't conform to my way of thinking or doesn't meet my expectations, I often get angry, pouting, or putting others down. This behavior affects many areas of our lives form relationships with family

members to religious and political opinions. How do you show your intolerance?

12) **Taking Things for Granted:** Often, we simply expect that everyone should recognize and accept that I am the center of the universe, and that my view of life is the only one. Our not being aware or concerned for anyone else is another way we take things for granted. How does this peak of your behavior?

13) **Impatience:** "I don't like to wait on or for anyone." "Things should have been done yesterday." "Lines in stores are terrible and I refuse to wait." How often has your impatience interfered with your relationships?

14) **Feeling Guilty:** There are many things that we may feel genuinely guilty about. However, we may use guilt feelings to feel sorry for ourselves until it becomes a way of life. We constantly kick ourselves and become martyrs. We may use these feelings as an excuse to drink or use chemicals.

II. **Life-Relationships:** In this area, give examples of how the following have interfered with your relationships and personal performance.

1) **Worry:** Always anticipating the future or going over the past allows us to ignore the present. We spend so much time and energy fretting about what may be or might have been, that there is no time left to live in the present. Share examples of how this has been true in your life.

2) **Envy and Greed:** When I'm so concerned about what others have and what I don't have, I'm really talking about my own self-centeredness. "I expect that I should have those things," "I expect to be powerful and different." Sometimes I wish I could drink like others without consequences. These characteristics often keep us out of touch with reality. Write examples of how this applies to your situation.

3) **Gluttony:** Not knowing when to stop eating, drinking, etc., we appear to be bottomless pits that eventually get sick from our won refusal to put limits on ourselves. How have you failed in setting and keeping limits in your appetites?

4) **Lustful Sexual Behavior:** So often our sexual behavior is a symptom of our distorted thinking. If we look at our sexual behavior closely, we may see our selfishness, our demanding ways, our misuse of people, and the violation of our own values regarding our sexuality. What are some examples of this from your life?

5) **Anger:** Anger takes many forms. Some are very obvious: fighting (physically and verbally), or putting people down. Others are more subtle: the quiet treatment, pouting, self-pity, depression. Often we use anger to cope with feelings of hurt, shame, sadness, fear and loneliness. How have you "acted out" your anger?

6) **Laziness:** To find energy to do things that are not number one on our list is often next to impossible. Even tasks that we might enjoy get done in a haphazard manner. We become sloppy in our work and sloppy in our relationships. We neglect our health. How has laziness affected your life?

III. **The Ten Commandments:** Whether you agree with these ten statements or whether you believe in them is not important. These Commandments can serve as a guide to check out our relationship with God (or Higher Power) and with other people. The first three examine our relationship with God and the next seven look at our relationships with others. When responding to each of these Commandments, answer them with examples of how you have **violated** the Commandment, not how you have kept it.

1) **You shall have no other Gods before Me.** Who or what has come first in your life? What was more important than anything to you: booze, pills, relationships, money, yourself?

2) **You shall not take the Lord's name in vain.** This goes way beyond swearing. It talks about how we are **phony** to God. We say we believe in God, yet, what would our living indicate? Do we only call on Him when we are in trouble? Do we make deals with God, "God, if you get me out of this jam, I promise I'll never drink again; or I'll go to church, etc..." How have you been phony in your relationship with God?

3) **Remember the Sabbath Day, to keep it Holy.** How willing have you been to set time aside to acknowledge a power greater than yourself? If you have been attending public worship, examine your motives. Has it been for show? To keep someone off your back? An obligation?

4) **Honor your Father and Mother.** Who has come first in your family? Would you want your family members to know everything you've done? How honorable have you been? How willing have you been to honor other's values? How have you responded to people you see "in authority"?

5) **Do not kill.** If you have killed someone, here is the place to share it. Also, consider the **relationships** you have killed. The love you have killed. The friendships destroyed. As addiction increases, relationships, out of necessity, deteriorate.

6) **Do not commit adultery.** Here consider your total sexual relationships. Who really comes first? Whose wants, needs and desires were looked after first? Don't get overly concerned with the legalities of adultery. Look at all of your sexual relationships. How has your sexual behavior exploited others? Is there self-deception involved?

7) **Do not steal.** Write about all the things you have stolen, including time. Time from your family, friends and employers. What about the stolen **love** that comes from wanting others to love you, but not being able or willing to live in return?

8) **Do not bear false witness against your neighbor.** When I want to keep myself believing that I'm "Okay," and "better" than I am, I might resort to talking about the "terrible" deeds of others. Also, if I talk long enough and loud enough about someone else, then maybe no one will see what I'm like.

9) **Do not covet your neighbor's wife/husband.** This takes us into our "If only" world. "If only I had a wife or husband like that," "If only I had someone to make love to like that." Constant daydreaming about how we would like life to be keeps us from reality. Our fantasies allow us to be great lovers, but out of touch with reality. How have you allowed your sexual fantasies to dominate your thoughts?

10) **Do not cover your neighbor's goods.** Like the 9th commandment, this is the dream world of material things.

"Things would be different if I had the money, the house, the car, the job that so and so does." This world of envy keeps us out of reality and "fans" our resentments and self-pity.

B. **Assets:** Our positive, constructive behavior; recovery in action. In this part of the guide, you are encouraged to examine your assets. What are you doing that helps you to feel good about yourself? How are you more self-accepting? Take all of your examples from the present, not from the past or from the future. This program teaches us to live **now**, 24 hours at a time. How are you doing helpful, positive things now? If you can specifically see what you **are** doing **now** that helps you like yourself, it should make it easier to continue acting in positive, constructive ways. **Keep your responses simple.** Remember, this is a simple program.

I. **New Life Qualities:** Saint Paul in the New Testament tells us that these three: faith, hope and love, are key ingredients to a new life. Examine how they are a part of your life now.

1) **Faith:** Who and what do you have faith in now? Your counselor, friends, God, the program?
2) **Hope:** What do you hope for now? Sobriety, felling worthwhile, renewed relationships?
3) **Love:** How are you able to demonstrate your love for others now? Are you concerned for others? Do you share yourself, your feelings?

II. **Everyday Living Experiences:** Look for the simplicity of living in every day events and activities. Keep your examples simple, down to earth, ordinary. It's the way you are currently living each day – not the way you should be living.

1) **Honesty:** Being able to be honest with oneself and others is a most difficult and yet a rewarding kind of behavior. In honesty, one learns the joy of accepting oneself and one's feelings. How have you experienced being honest?
2) **Admitting Mistakes:** The 10th Step talks about taking a daily inventory and when we were wrong to promptly admit it. This is

what happens when we surrender: we are able to admit our mistakes. How have you been able to admit your mistakes?

3) **Cheerfulness:** Are you able to see things to be cheerful about now? Do you see beauty in places you had forgotten about or had never considered before?

4) **Sharing:** To give of oneself without expecting something in return is an experience that can happen when we begin to break out of our self-centered and selfish ways. How does it feel to share with others, whether that be feelings or material things? How have you been showing your concern for others?

5) **Use of Time and Order:** Before we never seemed to have enough time and tings seemed to pile up. With order in our lives, we begin to use our time in more helpful, productive ways. How do you see this changing in your life?

6) **Getting the Job Done:** We often get good feelings about finishing a project we have started. Being responsible for doing even small tasks can give a person a real lift. What are some of the things you have completed? How do you feel about the present job you are doing of putting your life back together?

7) **Punctuality:** Being able to get to meals on time, to meetings when expected, suddenly gives a new dimension to responsibility. It's not too bad, and we feel good about ourselves. Is your life becoming more punctual?

8) **Courtesy:** How are you being helpful and polite? It may be a whole new way of life.

9) **Kindness:** In being kind to others, we are kind to ourselves. We may feel the bitterness of resentment lifting. How have you experienced being kind?

10) **Patience:** This may develop slowly. It may take a concentrated effort and a lot of use of the 3rd Step. How are you becoming more patient?

11) **Being Forgiving and Accepting of Others:** When we learn how to forgive others for not meeting our criteria, we can also begin to accept them for the Human Beings they are. This is a giant step in our own personal growth: accepting things and people who are less than perfect. What are some examples of "accepting the things I cannot change"? How am I becoming more tolerant?

12) **Balance:** As we begin to experience balance in our lives, the peaks and the valleys begin to average out. We strike a more happy medium between our seriousness and our humor, our work and our play. What are some examples of this out of your present situation?

13) **Acceptance of Self:** When we accept ourselves, life takes on new meanings for us. We feel good about ourselves. We experience a sense of serenity. We no longer feel we have to please people. We are "okay" with our limitations and potentialities. Being less afraid of what others might think or feel about us, we are willing and more able to care for and about others. In what ways have you experienced this? How are you feeling about yourself?

14) **Freedom from Guilt:** For all too long, we have used our guilt to whip ourselves and to feel sorry for ourselves. Have you begun to feel the freedom that comes from respecting yourself rather than hating yourself? Have you experienced this as a part of your growing in the program?

15) **Gratitude:** When we are grateful for our talents and abilities as well as our limitations, there is no need for false pride. How are you accepting both your strengths and weaknesses? Are you able to look to a power greater than yourself as the source of your recovery? Are you grateful for t help you have received from others?

III. **Attitudes:** In this section, for each category compare your previous attitudes with your present ones. If your attitudes in some areas have changed, you'll be able to see the change. If they have not, you may get a chance to see them more clearly. Remember, be specific, yet keep your responses simple.

1) To God
2) To myself
3) To my family
4) To my work
5) To others

IV. **Responsibilities:** To each category in this section, respond to: **Today I have been responsible:**

1) To God
2) To myself
3) To my family
4) To my work
5) To my Recovery Program (Treatment, A.A., N.A., Al-Anon, etc.)

V. My Plan for Recovery: In this section, write a short paragraph or two detailing daily disciplines that have become helpful to you. Also, answer this question: "What must I do and what am I willing to do, to maintain my sobriety and serenity?" (Eppley Treatment Center, 1978).

Epilogue

Dear Reader,

I have been given the Gift of a most wonderful life – certainly nothing I deserved. If I got what I deserved, I'd be sitting in prison, residing in an insane asylum, living homeless on the streets…or I'd be dead.

It's all truly a Gift from God and He has that same Gift reserved for you as well. You don't have to believe what I share in this book, but just for the heck of it, try it. I can't guarantee much, but I can guarantee that your life will change.

The older I get, the more I realize nothing is more important than friends and that's what we become – friends helping each other to allow God's blessings to manifest themselves in our lives.

Sincerely with Love,
Bill

About the Author

Bill K. is the Director of "MIRACLES" Chemical Dependence Treatment Center at the Siena/Francis Homeless Shelter. He is also the Assistant Executive Director of Siena/Francis. He developed the "MIRACLES" program 12 years ago. The program has grown into a 90-plus bed residential program that has experienced incredible success, with its main referral sources being its past graduates.

Bill holds degrees in Psychology, Sociology, Criminal Justice, a Master's degree in Counseling and Guidance and a Specialty Certificate in Adlerian Counseling. He is also a Licensed Mental Health Practitioner, Certified Professional Counselor, Licensed Alcohol and Drug Counselor and a Nationally Certified Hypnotist.

About My Dad

What can be said from me that would not sound biased for "Butch," my dad. Having stated this, I can share that this man helped show me the way to recovery and then, following his footsteps, into our profession. Since I personally know most of the details of the stories shared in this book, I can attest to the fact that if a person of my father's depth of addiction can find recovery through faith, then I believe anyone can – **anyone**. I find this book inspirational, both in my own recovery and as a professional. I know you will also.

Gary Keck
MS, LMHP, CPC, LADC
Keck Counseling Agency
Grand Island, NE

"From Addiction to Miracles" is a rare synthesis of inspiration, hope and spirituality. Written with brutal honesty and candor, Bill shares his hard-won wisdom gained from a life of addiction. It is a wisdom that he discovered for himself after a long, difficult journey. It eventually leads to this point of view and stage in his life where he has found his true meaning. His gift is helping others.

Bill's story will have a powerful effect on all who read it. Through his knowledge and experience, he has much to offer those with addictions who are searching for a better way of life. Thank you for this gift, Bill – I'm so proud of you.

Michelle A. Bauer
BS in Dietetics, AD in Rad Tech

Bill K. is a pioneer in making the connection between homelessness and substance abuse and successfully treating the homeless, chemically dependent client. His book and story are inspiring, not only for those struggling with addictions, but for all who struggle with life's habits, hang-ups and heartbreaks.

Chuck Cornwell
MA in Counseling, LMHP and United Methodist Pastor

I have been a friend and colleague of Bill K. since 1980, in the early days of his extraordinary recovery from chemical dependency. He went through a year-long counselor training program and also earned a Master's degree. Bill has directed three of the best known treatment center programs in Nebraska, including the famous Siena/Francis House in Omaha, which is a unique long-term residential treatment center for the poor. His charismatic personality, sensitivity and knowledge have inspired many unbelievable recoveries that could rightly be called "miracles." He is one of those good souls who have made God's work his own.

Father Jim Schwertley
St. Mary Magdalene Church
Omaha, Nebraska